# The Mountain Bike Book

Choosing, riding and maintaining the off-road bicycle

## Rob Van der Plas

Illustrated by the author

Bicycle Books – San Francisco

Copyright © Rob Van der Plas, 1984, 1988
Second edition, revised and updated 1988


Published by:
Bicycle Books, Inc.
P.O. Box 2038
Mill Valley, CA 94941

Distributed to the book trade by:
Kampmann & Co., Inc.
9 East 40th Street
New York, NY 10016

Printed in the United States of America

Cover photograph by the author
Frontispiece photograph by David Epperson / Bicycle Sport

Bicycle for cover photograph courtesy Fisher MountainBikes

Black and white halftone lithography by Repro Drafting Connection,
Ober Roden, W. Germany



**Library of Congress Cataloging in Publication Data**

Van der Plas, Robert, 1938 –
The Mountain Bike Book
Choosing, riding and maintaining the off-road bicycle
second edition, 1988
Bibliography: p. Includes index
1. Bicycles and bicycling, manuals, handbooks, etc.
2. Mountains, recreational use  ~ Recreation
3. Authorship - Handbooks, Manuals, etc.
I. Title                                            796.6
Library of Congress Catalog Card Number 83-51788

ISBN 0-933201-18-4 Paperback          /E

The first edition of *The Mountain Bike Book* appeared under
ISBN 0-933201-10-9

# Acknowledgments

Many people whose names don't appear on the title page contributed to this book. I would like to express my appreciation to those who have helped make this totally revised second edition of *The Mountain Bike Book* what it is. Several readers and experienced mountain bike riders have contributed their comments and suggestions. Others have made their mark through their critical letters or reviews of the first edition.

In particular, I would like to thank mountain bike pioneer Gary Fisher for taking the time to go through the manuscript for technical accuracy and to assure it is up to date. Finally, I would like to thank Paddy Monk for her thorough editing job and Christina for her contribution in collecting numerous useful bits of information from various sources, as well as many of the photographs reproduced in this book.

No doubt some deficiencies still remain. I invite readers, riders and reviewers to spare me neither their criticism nor their constructive suggestions. I shall make every effort to incorporate all comments received this way in the next edition.

# About the Author

Rob Van der Plas is a professional engineer and a lifelong cyclist who has ridden bicycles under all conceivable circumstances. In fact, he rode off-road long before the modern mountain bike was invented, riding on unpaved paths and rough trails in his native Holland and later in England. Though he does not consider himself amongst the pioneers of mountain biking as we know it today, he readily took to this wonderfully practical machine as soon as it was developed.

In this book he shares with the reader his own experiences as an off-road cyclist and his technical know-how as a bicycle engineer. He excels in disseminating the general cycling and engineering knowledge that allows truly competent mastery of the machine. The present volume is an extensively rewritten and updated adaptation of the book that first appeared in 1984.

Besides the present book, Rob Van der Plas has written numerous other books and articles on the subject of bicycling. His technical contributions regularly appear in specialized periodicals on both sides of the Atlantic. His earlier books include *The Bicycle Repair Book*, *Roadside Bicycle Repairs*, *The Bicycle Racing Guide* and the *Bicycle Touring Manual*, all published by Bicycle Books.

# Table of Contents

# Part I
# Choosing the Right Equipment

A fine Japanese built
machine to English specs,
mirrored in shallow waters.
Photo courtesy Muddy
Fox.

# 1
# The Mountain Bike Revolution

Suddenly, within the span of a few years, bicycling has gone through a revolution. An entirely new type of machine has not only appeared on the market, it has very nearly taken over. As recently as 1984, when the first edition of this book appeared, it was necessary to precede it with an explanation of what a mountain bike was. In fact, other books about the sport did not even mention the existence of this new iron steed. Yet today the mountain bike or ATB accounts for the great majority of all adult bicycles sold in the US and Canada, with Britain lagging not far behind. Suddenly, fat-tire bikes are everywhere.

Bicyclists have fallen in love with this rugged bike for all seasons. The industry has not stood still either: Mountain bikes and special components designed for them are big business, and today's machine makes the models of only a few years ago look antiquated by comparison. The mountain bike, it seems, has given the industry and the sport a new lease on life.

Mountain bike riding in the morning mist of the California coastline. (David Epperson photograph)

Indeed, it is hard not to be enthusiastic about this wonderful innovation. It helps novices become experts within record time and allows experienced cyclists to easily do things they had never thought possible before. The mountain bike is not only agile and rugged enough to go anywhere, it is also safer, more reliable and comfortable than any other bike I know. If you don't have one, you should. If you do, here's how to get the most out of this wonderful machine.

## About this Book
This book is devoted specifically to the mountain bike and the way it is used. All of its uses, not just for riding in mountains. Consequently, you will find quite a lot of advice related to propelling your bike on the road, in addition to specific recommendations for riding off-road. Though the mountain bike no doubt lends itself better to cycling off the beaten track than any other model, the undeniable fact is that this machine is also perfectly suitable to be ridden on regular paved roads.

The book comprises three parts and an Appendix. In Part I (Chapters 1

through 5), you will be shown how to select a bike, its accessories and other equipment, followed by advice on how to set it up initially. Depending on your preferences, your skills and the use to which the machine will be put, certain variants of the mountain bike and other items of equipment will be appropriate. Here you will learn how to select and adjust the best to match your needs.

Part II (Chapters 6 through 13) is devoted to the subject of handling the bike under all conceivable circumstances. Here you will be shown how to get the most out of the equipment you have. Various chapters deal with subjects ranging from bike handling to safety on and off the road, from steering to gearing and from cross-country touring to off-road racing.

Part III (Chapters 14 through 21) deals with the technical aspects of the mountain bike. I like to save this for last, since this material is not the easiest section of the book to read. Though some people want to know all the technical ins and outs, others will gladly put the book back on the shelf before things get this technical. For reference, the technical material will be useful to all, as it includes equipment evaluation guidance and repair instructions.

The Appendix contains some useful reference material that doesn't lend itself to prose treatment. Included are a frame sizing aid and a gearing table designed specifically for the kind of gearing and the wheel size typically found on mountain bikes. In addition, you will find here a troubleshooting guide to help you cure roadside problems, a list of addresses, a comprehensive bibliography and an extensive alphabetical index.

Compared to the first edition of this book, which was indeed the very first book to appear on the subject back in the spring of 1984, the contents of this edition are completely updated. In fact, the book has been entirely rewritten. All of the developments that have taken place since then are included here.

## Choice of Words

Before continuing, let me settle some points of terminology. In the first place, my use of the term *mountain bike* bears some explanation, if not justification. Other names have been suggested at times, including ATB (all terrain bike) and fat tire bike. As a matter of fact, both these terms are probably more accurate, since the majority of mountain bikes are not ridden in the mountains as much as the name would suggest. Just the same, mountain bike is the name most universally used, and who am I to argue with common usage?

Then there is the matter of spelling. Though this book is sold on both sides of the Atlantic, I shall use American spelling as much as my own tolerance for some of the local excesses allows. My British readers will find many words spelled in a slightly unfamiliar way: tire for tyre, aluminum for aluminium, center for centre, and so on. In addition, entirely different words are sometimes in use for the same concept in the two societies. Anticipating the resulting confusion, I have made every effort to explain the meaning of American expressions that differ from those used in Britain by more than the spelling alone.

Throughout this book, you will encounter references to manufacturers, brands, makes and models of certain products related to the subject. Some of these terms are registered brand names or protected trademarks, though they are not identified as such in the text. Their use here is for informative purposes only, for which reason these terms are not identified by the registration symbol.

The last point has to do with gender. Though my sympathy for sexual equality is as great as may reasonably be expected from a member of the male sex, my tolerance for linguistic concoctions like *he/she* and *man/woman*, or even compounds with *person*, is very low. And the meaning of *man* as a general term, referring to the entire human race, is neither discriminatory nor unreasonable in my eyes. Consequently, this will be the kind of language you will find here. I think it makes for better reading.

### Defining the Mountain Bike

To make sure we are all talking about the same thing, let me briefly summarize what to me makes the mountain bike — what distinguishes if from other bicycles. Simply put, fat tires and flat handlebars. But there's more to it. If that were all, the bike I used to

Fisher MountainBikes Mt. Tam. Typical top notch off-road bike built of fillet brazed Tange Prestige tubing and equipped with the finest components.

ride in Holland when I was a kid would be one, as would the 20 inch wheeled iron monster on which my children first learned to ride. On the other hand, my favorite mountain bike, which is equipped with dropped handlebars, would not qualify. So there must be more to it.

The mountain bike combines some of the best characteristics of several other machines, though it is clearly designed afresh. The fat tires have a tough tread for good traction on dirt, yet they are also light and can be inflated to a high pressure, resulting in remarkably little rolling resistance. The handlebars are wide enough to offer firm handling and flat enough to allow instant access to the brakes. At the same time, they are ergonomically designed, so they don't force you into a posture that is uncomfortable in the long run.

The frame is rugged, yet quite light. The wheels are driven via a fifteen-speed or eighteen-speed gearing system that allows you to take most inclines in your stride. Andthose gears

are easy to operate by means of thumb shifters. But this intriguing machine won't merely climb, it will go downhill safely, due to its balanced geometry. Finally, with the help of its special brakes, it can be stopped on a dime. Surely, this is a triumph of two-wheel ingenuity.

In subsequent chapters, we shall take a closer look at the characteristic features of the mountain bike and its components. You will learn that there are enough differences within the range of mountain bikes available to make some machines more suitable for certain purposes than others. Even more suitable, I should say, because basically even a very simple mountain bike will outdo virtually any other machine for many basic bicycling uses.

Perhaps the greatest positive aspect of the mountain bike is the appeal it has to those who have not previously felt very much at ease on a bike. Turned off by the poor performance and discomfort of the old American utility bike, yet not at ease with the drop handlebar ten-speed, these are the people whose bikes – if they had them at all – stood rusting away in a corner of the garage for many years. Young and old, men and women: all feel at ease on this machine.

Ten-speeds with drop handlebars were fashionable for a period of about 15 years. Like most experienced cyclists, I still relish mine, which I use preferably on paved roads. But the mountain bike has brought a form of equality to cycling. Now even the less skilled can buy a quality bike that matches their riding habits. Most likely, this is the bike that satisfies your needs, a bike that you can easily learn to handle as well as I can, even if you are a little older or a little less agile or athletically ambitious. At the same time, it is a bike that appeals to the toughest gonzos. Finally, fashion has caught up with common sense: here's the bike for everyone.

## A Little History

Although the mountain bike is a recent development, it already has a history that deserves to be told. In fact, its roots can be traced back to 1933. That's the year Ignaz Schwinn introduced the balloon-tired bicycle in the US. It had fat tires, but none of the other virtues of the modern mountain bike, except ruggedness. Heavy and indestructible, it soon became the standard for newspaper delivery and other forms of utilitarian cycling. Actually, it was meant to be a gag. Emulating the motorized vehicles of adult America, it offered the kids of America the closest approximation to a car – on two wheels and muscle powered, mind you.

Half a century later this curious design was to experience an unexpected revival. Cycling in America had gone through fits and starts, ups and downs. The ten-speed boom had come and gone. At least the ten-speed boom had finally allowed respectable adults to progress self-propelled, which had been unheard of for many years. Meanwhile, the younger generation's BMX bike had not only become a toy and a means of competition, it had also led to some surprisingly sophisticated technology.

But the mountain bike did not appear until the late seventies. Popular lore has it that it all started just North of San Francisco, on the slopes of Mount Tamalpais. Rather, I like to think of 'Mount Tam' as only one of several places where this development took place. What happened there, no doubt also happened elsewhere, and the timing can't have been far off.

As it was, men and youths made a sport of riding motorcycles down the rough slopes, which gave them hair-raising thrills. It was horrible in environmental terms, since it was not only noisy, it caused erosion, which disturbed the natural watershed. When the water district authorities got wind of it, they restricted motorcycles to paved roads. So the riders thought of other ways to get their thrills. They took to riding down the same slopes on bicycles, trucking back up the road in a pick-up.

They must have ruined a lot of bicycles that way, not to mention what they did to the environment, even without a motor. By and by, it became apparent what kind of bike would best stand up to this kind of use: that same fat-tired machine that Schwinn had introduced many years before. The Schwinn Excelsior, as it had been built from 1933 until 1941, turned out to be the ultimate bike for this kind of use.

A few problems remained, though. This bike's coaster brake had a way of overheating on the downhill, and the most famous stretch of Tamalpais slope is called Repack in its honor: after one descent, the heat had literally boiled the grease out of the bearings. You either had to repack the bearings with fresh grease or give up altogether. And then the idea of riding down, only to hitch a ride back up in a truck, seemed perverse to the true cyclist.

That was not the way Gary Fisher, one of the country's strongest cross-country bicycle racers, was going to play the game. Instead, he modified his fat tire bike to take derailleur gearing, thumb shifters and a seat post quick-release, so he could ride up as well as down. The idea caught on and soon some hillsides were swarming with reckless men and women trying to break their necks going down and busting their backs struggling up again.

Joe Breeze, one of the other named progenitors of the mountain bike according to the California gospel, went a step further. A framebuilder of some expertise, he decided to copy the geometry that seemed to lend the Schwinn Excelsior its superb uphill and downhill qualities onto a frame weighing quite a bit less. This was adapted to take the most suitable components available at the time, such as derailleur gears, cantilever brakes and motorcycle bars and levers. Essentially, the mountain bike was born. It just hadn't come of age yet.

Mountain bike pioneer framebuilder Tom Ritchie (David Epperson photograph)

This process was helped along by the next character to appear on the scene. Mike Sinyard is the name, an enterprising bicycle businessman from San Jose, California. Sinyard, through his company called Specialized, had proven in the past to have an excellent feel for what was good and how to sell it. This time, he engaged frame builder Tim Neenan, another member of the California breakneck crowd, to design a mountain bike frame that could be built in series, and specified the components that had proven themselves in actual use. Built in Japan for Specialized, this became the first production mountain bike: the Stumpjumper.

Now everybody with $ 750 to spare could have a mountain bike to call his own. Sinyard spent a fortune advertising this machine, and essentially pre-financed the entire mountain bike boom. This is one example of commercial pioneering. I suppose the Stumpjumper returned the cost of advertising it, but there is even less doubt that the whole mountain bike movement was established in the public mind as a result of this venture. Without it, there's a good chance the mountain bike's light would have remained under the bushel where many of its slightly off-beat devotees had a way of hiding it.

Not that others overlooked the mountain bike's commercial possibilities. For instance, there was the trio of Tom Ritchey, Gary Fisher and Charles Kelly. Before they went their separate ways as frame builder, bike businessman, and mountain bike guru, respectively, they set up what was probably the first commercially successful operation dealing only in mountain bikes. And then there were the many innovative frame builders who were also mountain bike riders, developing one refinement after the other.

Though Specialized clearly had a head start on them, the big American bike manufacturers were not caught napping. They did not waste much time before bringing out their own real or presumed mountain bikes. Some merely continued the junk they had been making for the cash-and-carry market in a form that made it look like a mountain bike. Others went into the business seriously. But most soon learned to do things right, especially those who had always been concerned with quality. Schwinn was there and even companies like Ross hired competent frame builders to design real mountain bikes that could be mass produced.

Foreign manufacturers didn't take long to catch on either. The Japanese and Taiwanese soon flooded the market with mountain bikes. As early as 1984, only two years after the introduction of the Stumpjumper, mountain bikes accounted for a third of the adult bicycle sales in the US. Today, the mountain bike has taken first place, regularly accounting for more than half of all adult bike sales.

Very soon special components, specifically designed with the mountain bike in mind, started to edge out the grab-bag of adapted items from other fields that had served so well in getting the show on the road. Manufacturers like Shimano and SunTour brought out comprehensive ranges of special mountain bike components. Encouraged by Japanese tax incentives, they keep improving their wares from year to year. Just when everybody thought the perfect mountain bike derailleur was here, they introduced indexed derailleurs. No sooner had the ideal brake been found, when the next generation of even better brakes appeared on the market. We're still improving the mountain bike; but yes, the mountain bike has come of age.

Simultaneously, an entirely new competitive sport had sprouted up. Off-road or mountain bike racing is now not only a popular participation sport, it also very soon became commercialized, with many of the major and minor manufacturers sponsoring their own teams. California and Colorado led the way, but soon enough also other parts of the US, Canada and Britain could boast literally dozens of mountain bike competitions and other off-road events each weekend.

### Mountain Bike Periodicals

Nowhere can the rapid development of the mountain bike be more clearly traced than in the remarkable increase in periodicals devoted to its use. Back in 1980, Charlie Kelly and Denise Caramagno first brought out their slightly outrageous *Fat Tire Flyer*. Initially, it was no more than a couple of mimeographed sheets of 8½ x 11, folded in the middle, filled cover to cover by the sponsors under various pseudonyms. It saw a rapid rise in readership within a very short time, and succeeded in obtaining enough advertising to pay the bills, despite its curiously dilettante appearance and editorial style.

Today, there are at least four national magazines specifically devoted to the mountain bike in the US alone. Printed on glossy paper, with lots of color photographs, professional layout, phenomenal advertising rates

Scott Nicol between a rock and a hard spot in Santa Rosa's Howorth Park. You don't have to do things like this with your mountain bike, but it may be interesting to see it can be done. (Photo Donald Favello)

and first class editorial material, they document the vigor of the sport and the industry. The mountain bike press has definitely arrived.

But that's not all. Look at the regular bicycle periodicals, and you'll notice that about half the space of some issues of such heavies as *Bicycling*, with a circulation of nearly 300 000, is devoted to mountain bikes and their use. The advertisers are not blind to it either. Even those who push items that have little bearing on just what kind of machine you ride, or in fact on whether you ride a bike at all, depict healthy adults grinding uphill or speeding down on a mountain bike. Yes, bicycling has gone through a revolution of late: the mountain bike revolution.

# A Close Look at the Mountain Bike

In the present chapter we will investigate the machine and its characteristics in some depth. This should help when it comes to making sure you know and understand what I or the established experts you encounter are talking about, whether in this book or elsewhere.

## Mountain Bike and Ten-Speed

There are at least two different ways of looking at the mountain bike: as a cyclist or as a novice. The former, generally used to other kinds of bikes, will be most intrigued by the differences between what he is used to and the mountain bike. The latter is perhaps less biased in looking at the machine. Instead, he needs guidance to distinguish specific parts and understand

Trek model 850 mountain bike with chrome-molybdenum steel frame and Shimano Deore component group.

the purpose of certain features. I shall make every effort to satisfy both categories of readers.

For the edification of both groups, the differences between the mountain bike and the conventional ten-speed will be highlighted here, meanwhile explaining what things are called to the uninitiated. This should help the experienced cyclist understand the mountain bike in terms of the features that distinguish it from earlier machines. At the same time this helps the novice appreciate what he is getting into.

Fig. 2.1 represents a typical mountain bike, while Fig. 2.2 shows a typical ten-speed with dropped handlebars. Most people refer to the latter as a racing bike, but that is about the same as referring to my kitten as a jaguar. Most of these machines are less used, or suited, for racing than

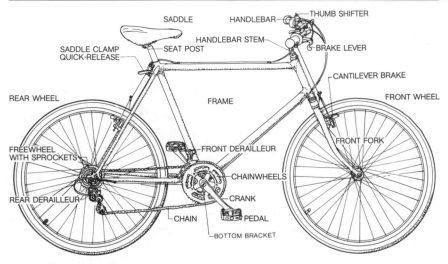

Fig. 2.1 The parts of the mountain bike

many make-believe mountain bikes are for mountaineering. Perhaps the fairest way of distinguishing the two breeds is by adopting the terminology introduced by the editors of the *Fat Tire Flyer*, the mouthpiece of the laid-back California mountain biking movement. They differentiate between Fat-Tire Bikes (preferably replete with capitals) and skinny tired bikes (lower case letters obligatory).

The drawing of the mountain bike is labelled with the names of the major components. The ten-speed drawing is only labelled with respect to those parts that are obviously different from their counterparts found on the mountain bike. Many of the major components pointed out here each comprise a number of distinct minor parts. It probably takes about 1000 distinct bits and pieces to make up a modern

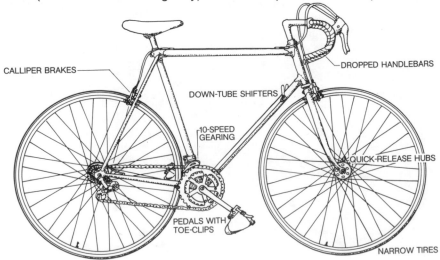

Fig. 2.2 The ten-speed bike

bicycle, though many of these parts are duplicates of one another. Take the chain, for instance: comprising about 600 parts, it must in fairness be noted that most chains only have five distinct types of parts – but then over a hundred of each.

The best way of appreciating and understanding the workings of the bike, is by looking at the various functional groups of components that make it up. Thus, I like to consider the following five categories: frame, steering system, seat, drivetrain, gearing system, wheels and brakes. These same groups will form the basis for looking at the technical aspects of the mountain bike in the chapters of Part III. For a quick initial overview of the machine, we'll consider these same groups here, as well as the accessories, to which Chapter 4 will be devoted.

## The Frame

As on any other bicycle, the mountain bike's frame forms its backbone. Usually, it is the only part actually made by the manufacturer whose name the bike bears. All other components are bought from component manufacturers and fitted to the finished frame in the bicycle manufacturer's plant. So, in fact, the bike manufacturer is typically more of an assembler when it comes to the rest of the bike. Of course, some bikes are not made in series, but are based on hand-built frames. These are generally the most exclusive and expensive machines.

The frame itself is made up of metal tubing, generally some type of steel, though more and more manufacturers offer aluminum frames these days. The frame's two major parts are the quadrilateral main frame, or forward portion, made up of large diameter tubing, and the double rear triangle, made up of thinner tubes in pairs.

The tubes of the main frame are referred to as top tube, downtube, seat tube and head tube, and their respective locations can easily be guessed from these names. The horizontal and vertical tubes of the rear triangle are called chain stays and seat stays, respectively. At the bottom, where down tube, seat tube and chain stays join, is the bike's heart, referred to as the bottom bracket. The tubes may either be connected by means of welded or brazed joints, or they may be held inside lugs, to which they are brazed. Technical details of this sort are explained in chapters 14 and 15.

The differences between a typical mountain bike frame and that of a ten-speed is a matter of dimensions and angles. The various tubes are longer, and the clearances are more generous, as is the distance of the bottom bracket above the ground. The angles between the horizontal plane and the seat tube and head tube are typically shallower, and some of the individual tubes, especially the down tube and the chain stays, should be of slightly greater diameter on the mountain bike. All these features make for a bike that is good natured and less sensitive to the irregularities of the terrain.

## The Steering System

The bike is steered by a combination of lean and front wheel turn. As will be described in more detail in Chapter 7, the steering system is essential to achieve both. It is comprised of the front fork, in which the front wheel is mounted, the handlebars with the stem that connects them to the fork, and the headset bearings with which the whole system is pivoted in the frame.

Clearly, the handlebars are characteristic on these machines: wide and flat. The stem should be a very sturdy model, to match the high stresses sometimes applied to the handlebars in rough terrain. The fork must be wide enough to accommodate the fatter tires and it had better be very strong. Its design has evolved quite a bit in recent years, as will be described in Chapter 16.

## Saddle and Seatpost

The mountain bike's saddle, or seat, is generally wider than that of the ten-speed bike, and usually more padded. All this to make up for the fact that most mountain bike riders tend to rest a greater portion of their weight on the seat.

The saddle is installed on a seatpost, which is attached in the frame's seat tube by means of a quick-release binder bolt. Loosening this bolt allows adjusting the height of the seat. On some older bikes an additional quick-release adjustment may be provided to vary the forward position of the saddle relative to the seatpost. These features allow quick response to variations in the terrain.

## The Drivetrain

This is the term for the system of components that carry the rider's pedalling force and motion to the rear wheel. Sometimes the gearing system is included in this group as well, though I prefer to treat it separately. So we have the pedals, installed on the cranks, turning in the bottom bracket bearings, with the chainwheels attached to the RH crank, and the freewheel with individual sprockets installed on the rear wheel hub.

Mountain bikes are often equipped with special cranksets, pedals and so on, designed specifically to match the rugged use these machines get and to provide a surer footing. Generally, the pedals lack the toeclips familiar from the ten-speed. The chain and several other components may be identical to those used on other bikes. The bottom bracket may be of a supposedly sealed variety to help keep out the worst dust and moisture.

## The Gearing System

Mountain bikes have at least 15-speed derailleur gearing – usually even 18-speeds. The derailleur gear system is based on the principle that the gear ratio is a function of the relative sizes of front chainwheel and rear sprocket over which the chain runs. The gearing adaptations are made by shifting the chain sideways while pedalling. That's done by means of shifting the front and rear derailleurs, or changers, to engage a particular combination of chainwheels and sprockets with different numbers of teeth. It's the same principle used on ten-speeds but is extended by using a third chainwheel in the front, in combination with five or six sprockets in the rear.

On virtually all mountain bikes, the gears are selected by means of thumb shifters installed on the handlebars within easy reach. In recent years, indexed shifting systems have become the standard in mountain bike gearing. These systems move the rear derailleur up and down through the various gears in distinct steps, rather than requiring tricky fine tuning. Chapters 6 and 19 deal with the practical and technical matters concerning the derailleur system.

## The Wheels

Ever since John Boyd Dunlop first introduced the pneumatic bicycle tire in the year 1887, the wheels have formed the bicycle's major suspension system. On a mountain bike, they perform that task more effectively than on any other kind of machine. They are fat for that very purpose. Keeping them at an adequate pressure will cushion the ride, while at the same time protecting the rims and tires against damage.

The tires, though always fatter than on most other bikes, come in several widths, varying from about 1.5 in to 2.2 in, with a nominal diameter of usually 26 in. The wider tires provide the best real off-road qualities, whereas those less generously dimensioned are more a reflection on a curious excess of economic protectionism. It stems from an excise tax dating back to the thirties, when US bike manufacturers rallied to prevent the importation of cheap bikes with the only size of tires the public wanted at the time. Just the same, these narrower tires will do just fine for some kinds of use.

The tires are mounted on metal rims. The latter had better be of aluminum, both to keep their weight down and to assure a reasonable

A complete mountain bike component group. The Deore XT 'gruppo' with Biopace chainwheel, indexed shifters, and Casette Freehub, to name just a few of the many bits and pieces that make up Shimano's top line.

braking performance even in wet weather. The rims are laced to the hubs in a net of wire spokes, just like any other bike wheel. The hubs on your mountain bike may be sealed against water and they may be attached by means of axle nuts, since that allows the use of solid axles. These are stronger than the hollow axles used for the handy quick-release hub attachments, which are nevertheless used more and more on mountain bikes as well as on ten-speeds these days. Chapter 20 contains all the detailed information you may ever want to know about mountain bike wheels.

### The Brakes

Mountain bikes need strong brakes. They are often ridden down steep slopes and they have to be stopped quickly and surely. Special mountain bike brakes are available in the form of cantilever brakes, special center-pull designs and roller cam models. All these, explained in detail in Chapter 21, are mounted on pivot bosses

that are attached directly to the tubes of fork and frame, for front and rear brakes, respectively. All of them must open wide enough to get the wide mountain bike tires through.

The brakes are operated by means of special handles, matching the flat handlebars installed on mountain bikes. These levers are within easy reach from the ends of the handlebars. As is the case with the ten-speed and other bicycles with caliper brakes, the levers and mechanisms are connected by means of flexible Bowden cables.

## Accessories
Mountain bikes may be equipped with a number of special accessories. These range from water bottle cages to luggage racks and various other extras that can be hung on any bike to advantage. Generally, these goodies must be designed specifically for mountain bike use, to match the different dimensions of such machines, as compared to other bikes. Chapter 4

Quick but effective chain lubrication using motorcycle chain lube. Just don't forget to clean the chain between applications, certainly if you ride in dusty terrain a lot.

contains additional information relating to many of the mountain bike accessories available.

## Care of the Mountain Bike
Perhaps the best way of becoming better acquainted with your mountain bike is by doing some of your own maintenance. Cleaning, adjusting and lubrication can easily be carried out on a regular basis with a very minimum of special tools and with little initial technical expertise. And what you learn while doing this work, pays off in terms of increased competence when riding the bike.

Even if you don't do anything else, at least clean and inspect your bike regularly. You may decide to let someone else take care of the actual maintenance, if you are so inclined. Clean the bike, preferably after every long ride, but at least once a month during the season, more frequently if you use it under really dusty or wet conditions. Do this immediately after the ride, rather than wait until the next time you need the bike, when you may find out it's not in operating order. Proceed as follows to clean your machine:

1. If the dirt is dry, take it off with a soft brush and a rag. If the dirt is wet or caked on, use a damp cloth or clean water to take it off. Just avoid getting lots of water and mud in the vicinity of the bearings, the cables and the chain. After the wet operation, clean it with a dry rag.
2. Use a small brush, or the corner of a rag wrapped around a narrow object, to get into all the hidden corners where the dirt is hard to remove. If it's necessary to remove greasy dirt, use a brush soaked in a mixture of ten parts kerosene (paraffin to my British readers) with one part motor oil. When the kerosene evaporates, the oil will re-

Take along at least these tools: screwdriver, tire irons, patch kit, Allen key, crescent wrench and pliers. In addition, you'll need a pump. On a long trip far from home, you should carry an expanded selection of tools and spares.

main in place to protect the components against rust. Don't get this mixture into the bearings, since it would dissolve the bearing grease.

3. Next, lubricate the various points indicated with an arrow in Fig. 2.3, using a spray lubricant. If you only ride the bike in dry weather and dry terrain, you may select a synthetic oil or a very thin mineral lubricant, such as WD-40. Otherwise, you'd be better off selecting a more waxy lubricant, such as motorcycle chain lube.

4. After cleaning and lubrication, check whether all the mechanisms are adjusted properly: saddle height, handlebars, brakes, gears. Make sure no bolts or nuts are loose or missing and that nothing is bent. Inflate the tires to at least the pressure indicated on the tire sidewall, but use quite low pressures for very soft ground.

Vine riding in the California wine country. (David Epperson/Bicycle Sport photograph)

You may refer any technical problems you encounter in this inspection to the bike shop. However, if you are more ambitious about maintenance – highly recommended for those who want to become really competent and at ease with their bikes – learn to carry out the adjustments yourself. The chapters of Part III of this book contain practical advice on such maintenance operations. Further instructions may be found in my *Bicycle Repair Book*, while my *Roadside Bicycle Repairs* will keep you out of trouble if some-

Fig. 2.3 Lubrication points

thing goes wrong while you are far from home and nowhere near a bike shop.

# 3

# Selecting the Right Mountain Bike

This chapter will familiarize you with the criteria that establish which particular mountain bike will best serve your needs. Clearly, it will be impossible to simply define what is 'the best mountain bike': it all depends on how you ride, what your needs are, and in what kind of terrain you will be riding most often.

There are enough differences to make the choice a challenging one. Various makes, models and sizes are available. And there are subtle details that at first escape the attention of the most careful observer who is not fully

Trek model 8000 mountain bike. It has a bonded aluminum frame and is equipped with Shimano's Deore components. The color scheme is that of the 1987 model but the specs are up-to-the-minute. You can get the same bike with black rims and Deore XT components, which are polished a little more elaborately.

prepared. But you will be prepared by the time you've worked your way through this chapter.

## The Price to Pay

Mountain bikes and machines that look just like them are available in prices that run the gamut from cash-and-carry junk to expensively crafted works of engineering art. Though almost every price has its justification in terms of the work and materials that went into the finished product, it would not be reasonable to suggest that the most expensive will be the best for every purpose. I know people who have had trouble with the most exclusive equipment they could (or could not) afford, while others have been perfectly satisfied with bargain basement machines.

My subjective evaluation of the general populace's mountain bike buying habits indicates there are three approaches:

☐ What is the best?
☐ What is the cheapest?
☐ What will be the most suitable for me?

Those who ask the first question, though probably wealthier, are not really any more sophisticated or smarter than those who try to find the answer to the second. It is my aim in this book to bring as many readers as possible into the category of the informed, those who ask – and attempt to answer – the third question. Only they will be likely to finish up with a bike that is best for them.

It all depends on your needs, the way you want to use the bike and your priorities. If your priority is conspicuous consumption, then the best and most expensive will be barely good enough, though you may not benefit one bit from all that expensive sophistication, perhaps even experiencing the drawbacks of such finesse more than its benefits. If you just want to ride around without any competitive intentions or interest in riding in difficult terrain, you may be well served with a cheap to medium priced machine. If you want to cycle faster than the next person, and have developed your riding skills, you may want the very lightest and sophisticated.

But don't expect miracles from the choice of equipment alone. The fancy bike will allow you to exploit your existing abilities, but you will benefit more from working on your skills before spending all your savings on that ultimate machine. It may take one to three seasons to develop your skills adequately, and if you splurge on that fancy machine now, it may be wrecked before you get a chance to benefit from its superior qualities.

Most people who buy their first mountain bike, and quite a number of those who have had such machines before, don't do so in order to com- pete with the gonzos who make a living blazing their trail up and down the steepest mountains. They want a bike they are at ease with. It should be the right size, comfortable enough to ride for hours, light and agile enough to be handled easily, and priced somewhere within your financial possibilities. Yes, it can be done – let's see how to go about it.

**The Right Size**

Whatever the make, model, type, color or price, your bike should be of the right size to match your physique. If it's the wrong size, the best bike is worse to ride than an otherwise inferior model of the right size. Here you will find guidelines for making sure you get a bike that fits.

Bicycle sizes are generally quoted as the length of the seat tube, between the center of the bottom bracket and some point at the top. Yes, some point. Traditionally, in the English-speaking world this upper point has been defined as the top of the seat lug. More and more manufacturers of mountain bikes refer to the more logical location represented by the centerline of the top tube. Some are even smarter, quoting the height of the top tube above the ground. The difference between the first two designations may be anywhere from 15 mm to 30 mm (⅝ to 1¼ in), depending on the seat lug detail, while the third size also accounts for the angle of the seat tube and the height of the bottom bracket above the ground. Fig. 3.1 illustrates this and the other critical dimensions of the bike.

The correct frame size will be a function of the length of your legs. As a guideline, you can refer to Table 1 in the Appendix. It gives suggested nominal frame sizes as a function of the inseam leg length, as measured in Fig. 3.1.

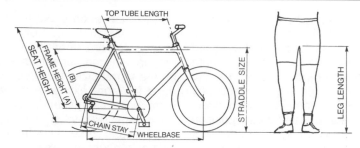

Fig. 3.1 Frame size determination

Fig. 3.2 Straddle height

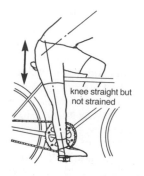

Fig. 3.3 Seat height determination

Obviously, the surest way to find out for yourself is by trying out some bikes. Certainly if you intend to use the mountain bike for its original purpose, namely to ride off-road, the frame should be on the small side, relative to the sizing practice customarily recommended for other bicycle types. Straddle some bikes in the shop and select one on which you retain up to 7.5 cm (3 in) of crotch clearance when your feet are flat on the ground. While straddling the bike, raise the front end. On the right size bike, you should be able to lift the front wheel about 12.5 cm (5 in) off the ground without discomfort, as illustrated in Fig. 3.2

In addition to being able to straddle the bike when it is standing still, it should of course fit you when riding it. That is a matter of reaching the pedals from the saddle in the right manner. Fig. 3.3 shows how you should sit and reach the pedal to try it on for the correct seat height. Don't pedal it that way when cycling, though. Instead, keep the front of the foot centered on the pedal, rather than the heel.

Once you have established the right saddle height, mark the seat post at the point where it protrudes from the seat tube. Then undo the binder bolt and pull it out to check its length. There should be at least 2½ in of the seat post below the point you just marked. If there isn't, you either need a different bike or a longer seat post. Insist on it, since a seatpost that is not held in the frame by at least that much is not safe.

**The Length of the Frame**
Then there is the length of the bike to consider: how far is the saddle from the handlebars and what is the distance between the wheels. Customarily, the length is quoted as the top tube

length, measured between the center-lines of head tube and seat tube. Typically, most manufacturers offer a fixed relationship between seat tube length and top tube length. Of course, the critical dimension is also affected by the size of the handlebar stem extension and the relative forward position of the saddle with respect to the seat post.

To find a bike of the right length, start off with the saddle placed in the middle and the handlebars at the same height. Seated on the bike, you should be able to sit relaxed, dividing your weight between handlebars and saddle. You should not feel uncomfortably strained. The other extreme, with the hands too close to the body, rarely occurs, since most bikes seem to be rather on the long side. Just the same, it's possible, e.g. if your upper body or arms are long relative to your leg length.

**Sex and the Bicycle**

With respect to the way bicycles fit their riders, there are some differences between the typical female and male physiques. For any given total body height, the woman tends to have proportionally longer legs and a shorter torso. Applied to bicycle sizing, that translates into a shorter top tube for the same size frame. I can't tell you what is the right top tube length for each frame size for either sex, since neither men nor women come in standard proportions. Comparing different bikes of the same size, women will generally be happier with a frame that has a shorter top tube. Replacing the handlebar stem with a longer or shorter model, if available, may also do the trick.

There are a number of special components on the market to suit the particular needs of women better than what is standard. Such items include wider saddles, narrower handlebars

and shorter reach brake levers. The smart manufacturers offer either special women's versions, or at least proportional component sizing based on the frame size. This is often only done for more exclusive models. At least one manufacturer, Georgena Terry, specializes in bicycles for women and recently introduced a women's mountain bike.

Let's keep in mind that people are not standardized into male and female stereotypes. Some men will do better with one or more of the features more typically intended for women, and vice versa. Thus, some men have a pelvice that is as wide as some women and the wider women's saddle would be appropriate for them. Evaluate your own physical characteristics critically before buying a bike, so you know what to look out for. Then try out several different models just as critically, and don't rush into buying something before you are sure it fits and suits you.

**Wheel Size**

Virtually all mountain bikes are equipped with what is referred to as 26 in wheels. That's the approximate overall outside diameter with inflated tire. There are 26 in tires in numerous different widths. On mountain bikes they may vary all the way from 1.5 to 2.2 in.

Not everybody needs the widest tires. If you ride on roads most of the time, rarely getting into loose dirt, sharp boulders, mud or snow, you may be perfectly happy with say 1.5 or 1.6 in tires. The wider tires are the solution for really rough terrain or loose dirt, mud and snow. Generally, bikes are designed with a particular tire size in mind, so it is wise to select a bike that is equipped the way you want it, rather than modifying it later.

However, since virtually any tire width can be installed on the same rim, it is often possible to replace the narrow tires with wider models for no more than the cost of the tires. Of course, that only works if the frame clearances are adequate. The narrow tires can essentially always be replaced by 1.75 and 1.9 in wide models. For more details on tires and wheels, you are referred to Chapter 20.

### Climbers, Descenders and Runners

The first mountain bikes were designed to do nothing else quite as well as descending from steep hills. That was mainly achieved by keeping the wheelbase – the distance between the wheel axes – rather long. Since then, different geometries have been introduced by various and sundry manufacturers. Many claim the most curious advantages of certain features. Here is a summary of the most important points.

### Chainstay Length

Short chainstays – on which the distance between the centerlines of the bottom bracket and the rear wheel is 17 in or less – are reputed to give a bike magic climbing ability. Don't believe it. The fact is that these short chain stays avoid sway of the rear end when applying force to the pedals. So that's good for people who grind their way up in a gear that is too high. The disadvantage of this design is that it places the rider's weight rather far back, assuming a given angle of the seat tube relative to the horizontal plane. This actually makes it harder to climb very steep inclines, since the front end will tend to lift off. Great for racing down though.

### The Way You Ride

To give you some pretty general rules of thumb, beginners should look for a bike that is built more for comfort than for speed. That means one with relatively shallow frame angles: the head tube should make an angle of 68–71° relative to the horizontal. Due to some geometric relationships, that will also mean the bike will be a little on the long side. It will not respond as directly to your steering and accelerating efforts. On the other hand, it won't be quite as scary to ride either.

More experienced riders may be well served with a shorter and steeper machine. Frame angles of 72° or more are not unusual in this category. These fast and agile bikes will have a wheelbase of around 106 cm (42 in) or less, while the better bikes for novices will be longer, say 110 cm (43–44 in).

The shorter and steeper bikes are not only more agile, they are also rather rough to ride if you are in the habit of resting on the saddle with all your weight. Experienced riders don't: they divide their weight between pedals, handlebars and saddle. You too can get a short and steep bike once you've learned to do that. Some people learn within a single season, while others never catch on.

Mountain bike, English style. This early Cleland Range Rider was superb for muddy terrain. (Photo Courtesy Geoffry Apps)

If you are going to ride in really difficult terrain and make your bike suffer, you'd better get one that stands up to that kind of abuse. Not all mountain bikes are really built to last that way. Many are perfectly good for the kind of use 90 percent of the riders give their bikes, but these probably do not stand up to rough abuse. Such less robust machines are often a little lighter than other bikes in the same price category. Otherwise, lighter bikes tend to be more expensive.

Typically, mountain bikes that are really designed for hard riding are built of larger diameter tubing than used for ten-speeds. This applies especially to the down tube, the chain stays and the fork. Taking a look at various models, and asking the right questions in the bike shop, will usually allow you to get a machine that matches your kind of riding. Be fair on your pocketbook: there is no need to get an indestructible, expensive machine if you don't really need one. Don't be tempted by what is supposed to be the best. Even the best is relative: you want to choose what is best for *you*.

## Carrying Luggage

If you will be carrying luggage at some time, whether on long tours, to deliver newspapers, or to do the grocery shopping, you will need a bike that lends itself to that purpose. It should either have racks installed, or at least have the appropriate attachments, so you can install them at a later time. Most rack manufacturers nowadays copy the standard attachment details pioneered by Jim Blackburn.

If your bike has the bosses front and rear to match those racks, you'll be well prepared to install just about any manufacturer's racks, including Blackburn's own, which are the acknowledged leaders. If not, all is not lost, since it is possible to attach racks with the aid of provisional clamps and the like, as will be shown in Chapter 4. This is really only second best, but it may be the only choice left if you did not get the ultimate bike in the first place.

## Gearing Choices

Virtually all mountain bikes sold these days have indexed gearing systems. That means there are fixed positions for the various gears, at least on the rear derailleur. That's a nice feature, but there are other things to consider when it comes to gearing as well. In the first place, there is the number of gears. I suggest being satisfied with a 15-speed model in preference to one with 18 speeds, not to mention 21-speed systems. This applies in particular if you will be cycling in rough terrain and if you do not want to spend a lot of time straightening out your rear wheel, as will be explained in Part III.

Then there are the recently popular off-round chainwheels, such as the Shimano Biopace, which are often used on mountain bikes. These provide a better distribution of effort if you pedal at a low pedalling rate with high pedal force. More experienced riders have developed a riding style that is based on spinning fast, while exerting relatively low force. For these riders, the off-round chainwheels are of little use. I suggest learning to ride properly, rather than buying the equipment that is designed to compensate for your inefficiency.

## Materials and Construction

Many parts of the bike are of aluminum alloy these days. Rims, cranks, chainwheels, brakes, hubs and seatpost are generally made of aluminum on a bike of any quality. But more and more, also the bicycle's major component, the frame, is being offered in versions made of aluminum.

Aluminum bikes can be excellent – but so can steel bikes be. The former are generally a little lighter and often more expensive than comparable steel bikes. The major disadvantage is their intangibility: many of these machines haven't been on the market long enough to assure that they will stand up to the kind of abuse they may get.

Their other, and more practical, disadvantage is the fact that some standard components may not fit on them as easily as they do on steel frames. The reason lies in the need to use larger diameter tubing, as explained in Chapter 14. Attaching standard components to such an oversize tube may be tricky. But it would be unfair to call aluminum bikes inferior. Just the same, amongst moderately priced production bikes, I prefer those with steel frames, if such a subjective opinion is worth anything to you.

Steel frames can be made one of several ways: lugged or lugless, and lugless either with welded or with brazed joints. Though this will be discussed in more detail in Chapter 15, I should say a few words about it here, since you may be confronted with such a choice when buying a bike. The habit of building without lugs grew out of necessity, since initially no lugs were available to fit the oversize tubing diameters used on good mountain bike frames.

Since those days, lugs in the appropriate sizes have been introduced, yet lugless bikes have not disappeared. At the time of this writing, the best value amongst low-budget bikes from Japan and Taiwan seems to be in lugged frames. Lugless brazed frames (smooth joints) are the prettiest and the most expensive. They are also quite rigid, but not necessarily the lightest, due to the extra weight that goes into the brass fillets. Fig. 3.4 illustrates typical joints of the three different kinds.

Shimano Biopace crankset. The 'squarish' chainwheels allow less accomplished riders to get the most out of their low pedalling speed. Several other manufacturers make similar claims for their oval chainwheels. Note where the label goes: that's the way it will fit back together if you ever disassemble the unit.

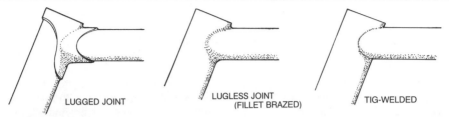

LUGGED JOINT  LUGLESS JOINT (FILLET BRAZED)  TIG-WELDED

Fig. 3.4 Joint types

What's best? If you are interested in being the fastest kid on the block and don't care how much you spend and how long your bike lasts, by all means get a bike with an expensive lugless, brazed frame. I must admit it is a delight to ride such a machine, which feels like an extension of your own body, rather than something with noticeable inertia of its own. On the other hand, my budget forces me to look for things I can afford, and within that range, some of the lugless welded frames are just right for me.

# 4
# Other Equipment

In addition to the mountain bike itself, you'd do well to get some other items, which will be introduced in this chapter. This other equipment is of two kinds: things to install on the bike, and things to wear or take along that have nothing to do with the bike as such. Thus, we'll also spend some time talking about the clothing to wear, as well as items that are typically referred to as bicycle accessories.

### Mountain Bike Accessories

While you are at the bike shop buying your mountain bike, consider a few other essentials. They'll run up the price of your purchase quite a bit, but you won't regret it, since these items will help you get more use out of your machine. Not all the things mentioned here must be bought right away, but it's good to know what's available. We'll take the essentials first.

Many of these regular accessories, such as racks, bags and fenders, are available in special versions for mountain bike use. This is not excessive diversification, since the dimensions,

characteristics of design, and the different way the machine is used, dictate distinct dimensions, designs and materials for the accessories as well.

### Lock

Sadly enough, bicycles are a lot harder to hold on to than they are to ride. The best lock is barely good enough to keep up with the determination of those who make a living by taking what belongs to others. Since society at large has not caught on to the high price of quality bikes, the act of stealing one is regarded merely as petty theft, and thus relatively riskless to the perpetrator.

Lock your bike whenever you're not riding it, in any place, including your own basement. And don't just lock it by itself but to something strong and firmly embedded. The best locks available are the large U-locks, such as those made by Citadel and Kryptonite. For your mountain bike, the largest model is about the right size. Lock at least the frame and one wheel to a firmly embedded object over

This is the way to lock your mountain bike: using a U-lock, such as this Kryptonite model, locking wheel and frame to a fixed object.

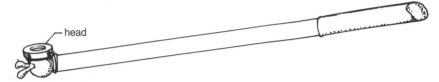

Fig. 4.1 Hand pump

which the lock can't be lifted; preferably also remove the other wheel and
lock it up too.

### Pump

Don't rely on the air supplied at gas
stations. You'll save a lot of time,
trouble and frustration if you carry
your own pump. Check the pressure
before you set out on a ride and inflate
the tires if necessary: at least 60 psi if
you travel mainly on paved roads,
about 45 psi if you ride on rough and
rocky terrain, and about 25 psi if you
travel mainly on soft or muddy ground.
This assumes a rider of average
weight: the pressure should be up to
five psi higher or lower if you're particularly heavy or light, respectively.

The tire inflation pressure greatly affects the bike's rolling resistance. Harder tires roll better, assuming a
smooth surface. Higher pressures
also protect both tires and rims
against damage from protrusions on
rough surfaces. Only on soft ground
should the pressure be quite low, so
the wheels don't get bogged down.

Pumps come in several types. For
home use, the big stand pump with integral pressure gauge is best, but on
the bike you need a more portable
model, shown in Fig. 4.1. Either type
should have a connector or head to
match the tire valves, which in turn
come in two or three types, shown in
Fig. 4.2. The most common valve
types are Schrader and Presta, while
the Woods or Dunlop valves are not
very widely used in the English-
speaking world. The Schrader valve is
the same thing found on car tires and

Fig. 4.2 Valve types

Fig. 4.3 Pressure gauge

is best inflated at the gas station. It
has an internal spring that makes it
hard to pump up by hand. The Presta
valve has a little screw that must be
undone before inflating, and tightened again afterwards.

Make sure your pump matches the
valves on your bike. When not in use,
install it along one of the frame tubes.
The frame-fit pump will either fit between the top tube and the bottom
bracket or along the top tube (if a peg
is installed just behind the head tube),
while other models require a mush-
room clamp at the upper end. In addition to a pump, I suggest you get a
pressure gauge, shown in Fig. 4.3. It
will take the guesswork out of inflating
to the right pressure.

### Water Bottle

Certainly for longer rides in hot weather, a water bottle, shown in Fig. 4.4
together with its cage, is an essential
accessory. Make sure there are bos-

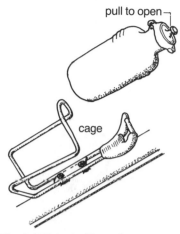

Fig. 4.4 Water bottle and cage

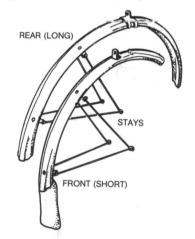

Fig. 4.5 Fenders

ses to mount at least one bottle cage on the bike. The way you use the bottle has to be learned too: pull the tip out while it is still in its cage. Then remove the bottle and squeeze it to squirt a jet of water into the mouth — you're not supposed to suck but to squirt.

## Fenders
These things are called mudguards in England and are shown in Fig. 4.5. Whether called fenders or mudguards, most inhabitants of the US wouldn't be seen dead with them on their bike. Fenders are useful in rainy weather, so it makes sense to install them if that is often the case in your part of the world. Get a model with a mud flap (or add your own) at the bottom of the front fender, which stops the rain from splashing right into your shoes. Fenders can be a problem in particularly muddy terrain, since the mud builds up inside them, eventually hindering more than they help.

### Luggage Carrying Equipment
Make sure your mountain bike can be equipped with racks, i.e. that it has at least the eyelets and lugs to which a rack can be installed. If you go touring with a lot of gear, you'll want racks both front and rear. Otherwise, a rear rack will generally be adequate.

You may also carry your gear in some kind of bag, attached either to the bike or the rider. Some possible bags are illustrated in Fig. 4.6: the backpack, the handlebar bag, the frame pack and the saddle bag. I prefer the latter, which is very popular in Britain, though Americans seem to prefer handlebar bags. Handlebar bags negatively affect your bike's handling and make it hard to mount most headlights. They are handy for relatively light items to which you want ready access. Make sure the handlebar bag is firmly supported from the top and restrained at the bottom by means of elastic shock cords.

### Bicycle Tools
Buy the essential tools right away. If nothing else, at least get a tire patch kit, a set of three tire irons (tyre levers in Britain), a small screwdriver to adjust the derailleurs, and a crank tool to tighten the crank. I usually carry a more complete tool set, which also includes various wrenches. You may also take along a tube of waterless

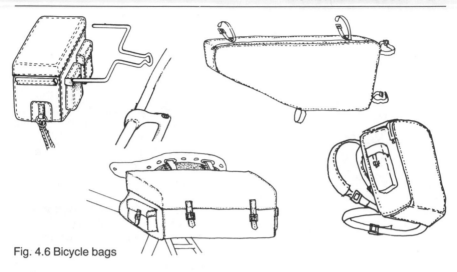

Fig. 4.6 Bicycle bags

hand cleaner and a rag to wipe your hands off when you've finished fixing the bike.

Certainly for longer tours, it will be wise to carry some additional tools and spares to match the various parts on your bike. Wrap the tools in a rag and keep them all together with an elastic band, or sew a pouch as illustrated in Fig. 4.7 to keep them together and organized. Ask at the bike shop when you buy the bike which tools you are likely to need, or establish that yourself.

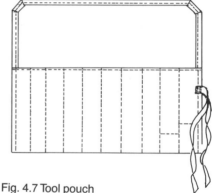

Fig. 4.7 Tool pouch

### Clothing
Even if you don't intend to dress up like Greg LeMond or Rebecca Twigg, there are a few items of bicycle wear that may benefit everybody. Besides, there are some considerations in the selection of clothing that should be applied whatever kind of clothing you wear when riding your bike.

Fig. 4.8 shows some of the typical things bicyclists wear, though one of the most essential, the helmet, is not depicted there. These items are all designed with the motion and exposure typical for cycling in mind. Thus, all garments are flexible and light, covering the areas of contact between bike and rider with some form of protection, and are made of materials that absorb perspiration. Keep these points in mind when buying clothing to wear when riding your mountain bike.

In general, mountain bikers will do well to consider the risk of falling off their bikes. For that reason, I suggest you wear long sleeved tops and long legged pants, rather than T-shirts and shorts. It will be even better to wear two (thin) garments over the top of one another, since in case of a spill the two layers will slip over one another, rather than taking chunks out of your skin. The hands could use the protection of a pair of gloves.

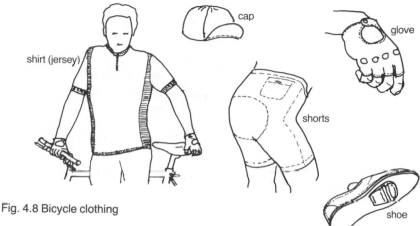

Fig. 4.8 Bicycle clothing

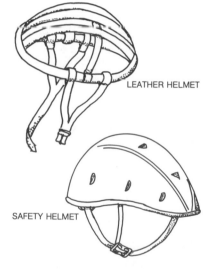

Fig. 4.9 Helmets

### Helmet.

A bicycle helmet is the first and most essential item of bicycle wear that I suggest you get. Not one of the old padded hairnets, but a real energy absorbing model, usually referred to as *hard shell*. In Chapter 9 you will get some of the background information about the need for head protection. For the time being, it should suffice to know you will be better prepared if you wear one. Don't just put it on top of your head, but buckle it up, if you want it to do you any good. Fig. 4.9 shows the energy absorbing safety helmet and the 'hairnet'.

There is one situation where I regularly take my helmet off. In hot and humid weather it becomes unbearable to cycle up steep inclines wearing a helmet. I perspire a lot under these circumstances. As long as the perspiration on your head gets a chance to evaporate, you may feel quite comfortable. But since you'll be going at a low speed, even the most intricately designed helmet ventilation system will not carry off your perspiration from under that helmet. You may also want to take the helmet off under those circumstances – and put it back where it belongs as soon as you reach the top, to protect you on the more dangerous way down.

### Shoes

All good bicycle shoes have a stiff sole, to better divide the pedalling force over the entire foot and deliver it to the pedal. For mountain bike use, you may get light half boots or shoes with stiff rubber soles, since you will probably not be using the cleats that are typical for racing bikes.

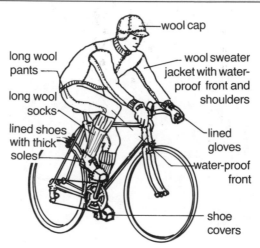

long wool pants

long wool socks

lined shoes with thick soles

wool cap

wool sweater jacket with water-proof front and shoulders

lined gloves

water-proof front

shoe covers

Fig. 4.10 Cold weather gear

### Cold Weather Wear

Mountain bikes are great machines for riding even when the weather is a little cooler. Wear something akin to the gear depicted in Fig. 4.10. Once more, several thin and flexible layers, preferably of materials such as knitted polypropylene or wool, are preferable to one layer of a thicker fabric. Watch out in particular for wind protection: the outer layer should be very closely woven, especially in the areas that face forward.

### Rain Gear

Many cyclists never venture out when it rains. I don't relish rain either, but I think it is smarter to prepare for the possibility of rain than to stop riding altogether when there is only the slightest chance of rain. In areas like Britain and the Pacific Northwest, nobody would get much cycling done if they didn't accept the possibility of getting wet. Cyclists there take the necessary clothing to fend it off, and so should you, wherever you live.

The problem with most rain garments is that if they are really waterproof enough to keep the rain out, they also trap perspiration in. Con-

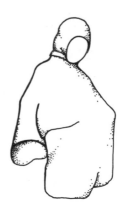

Fig. 4.11 Rain cape

Fig. 4.13 Spats

Fig. 4.12 Sou'wester

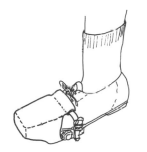

Fig. 4.14 Pedal covers

sequently, you may still get wet and uncomfortable. Avoid this problem by selecting rainwear made from the kind of fabric that keeps rain out but allows water vapor through. Examples of such fabrics are GoreTex and Tenson, though there are others.

For the top, I suggest using a cape, shown in Fig. 4.11, although you may prefer a jacket. If your helmet has those silly cut-outs and air scoops, you may also need a helmet cover. People who don't wear helmets (in many countries the risk of being ridiculed unbearably for wearing one is greater than that of cracking your skull if you don't) may keep their heads dry by means of a Sou'wester, illustrated in Fig. 4.12 This type of headgear is particularly practical,

An unidentified competitor drawing water at the Whiskeytown Downhill Race in Northern California. (Photo Donald Favello)

since it keeps the rain from running down your back.

To keep the legs dry, I prefer spats to full rain pants or leggings. Spats are covers for the front of the legs, as illustrated in Fig. 4.13. At the bottom, they should continue to cover the top of the shoes. To keep your feet dry, you may either use pedal covers, as illustrated in Fig. 4.14, or you may wear plastic overshoes. Personally, I find the most effective way to keep comfortable is by putting thin polythene bags over the socks, inside my shoes. In really muddy terrain, I go one step further and wear rubber boots, cut off just above the ankles.

# 5

# Fitting the Bike to the Rider

In this chapter you will learn how to set up the equipment you have so that it serves you best. To do this effectively, you should have selected a bike of the right size, as described in Chapter 3. The correct set-up and the initial riding posture will be explained here, which will in turn allow you to reap maximum benefit from the advice contained in Part II, which is devoted to handling the bike.

### Riding Posture
Whether you are cycling cross-country or on paved roads, the conventional idea of a comfortable position may have to be reconsidered. Though bicycle racers have long known that they are most comfortable in a relatively low, crouched position, most other cyclists – whatever kind of bike they ride – sit upright. That may be fine for folks who travel only short dis-

Providing you have the right size bike, every rider can adjust his mountain bike for proper posture and optimum riding comfort.

tances in town or make minor excursions at low speed in easy terrain. However, the serious mountain bike rider can learn something about posture from more experienced riders. The fact that you will probably have difficult terrain to handle makes this even more important.

Fig. 5.1 shows the three basic kinds of riding postures for comparison: upright, inclined and fully crouched. The cyclist who rides in the upright position may well be convinced this is the only comfortable way to ride a bike. As I look out of my window, I see at least thirty people cycling by in this posture each hour. Those who are going north have a very slight uphill – only a 1 % slope. All are working hard, you can tell by the strained expression on their faces, their cramped movements and their abysmally slow progress. Every now and again another type of cyclist comes by. Passing the others at twice their speed, and obviously more relaxed, these are the ones who ride in either a deep incline or in a fully

crouched position. Some ride racing bikes, others mountain bikes, but what distinguishes them is not their equipment but their posture.

There are, of course, also other reasons why they are going faster and suffering less, but the first and most important step towards this more comfortable style is their different riding posture. In the lower position, the rider's weight is divided more evenly over handlebars, saddle and pedals. Firstly, this reduces the pressure on the rider's buttocks. Secondly, it allows the relaxed fast pedalling technique so essential for long duration power output, as will be explained in Chapter 6. Thirdly, it enables them to bring more force to bear on the pedals when needed.

Finally, it can reduce the wind resistance, which is a major factor in cycling, especially when travelling fast or against the wind. As you can tell from Fig. 5.2, the cyclist's frontal area is crucial to the wind resistance, and is much less in the more inclined positions, which is reflected in the power required to ride the bike at the same speed.

Strangely enough, many people to whom the advantages have been demonstrated, nevertheless insist on riding in the upright position. They bring all sorts of arguments, ranging from, "That's only for racing" to, "That is terribly uncomfortable" or, "You can't do that on a mountain bike." They are fooling themselves. In reality, they are less comfortable, whatever they think, and have to do more work to cover the same distance or to proceed at the same speed. Get accustomed to the right posture early in your cycling career, and you'll be a more effective cyclist, one who gets less frustration and more pleasure out of the pursuit.

Within the general range of comfortable positions, there are enough vari-

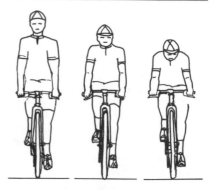

Fig. 5.1 Riding positions and frontal area

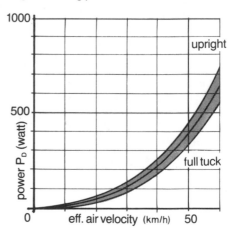

Fig. 5.2 The effect of frontal area

ations. This makes it possible to adapt to different terrain conditions and gives you the chance to vary your position from time to time. The latter helps avoid the numbing effect when pressure is applied in the same position for a long period of time.

The following sections describe just how the saddle and the handlebars should be adjusted to achieve the basic relaxed position that is shown in Fig. 5.3. This posture is worth looking into a little closer. Study the proportions. Unlike the person riding a bike with drop handlebars, the mountain bike rider cannot provide much variation by holding the handlebars at different points. Instead, he has to bend adapt to the terrain off-road, it should also be set for cycling on normal roads and relatively level ground. The saddle should be adjusted so that the leg can be almost stretched without straining the knee, which would cause excessive force and rotation at the joint. With the pedal in the highest position, the distance between the pedal and the saddle must be such that the knee is not bent excessively. Once this has been set, the correct crank length assures that the latter condition is also satisfied.

I shall describe a simple method of establishing the correct seat height. It is good enough for preliminary set-up and the first thousand miles of cycling. Your ultimate seat position may require additional fine-tuning, based on your subjective long-term comfort. On the other hand, in the vast majority of cases this technique will lead to a satisfactory seat position.

Fig. 5.3 Relaxed position

The simplest way of finding the correct level-ground seat height is illustrated in Fig. 5.4. It is a trial and error method and is easy to carry out without help. Wear the shoes you will be wearing when cycling. Place the bike next to a wall or post for support when you sit on it. The crank should be pointing down in line with the seat tube. Adjust the seat up or down, following the adjustment procedure below, until you can rest the heel of your shoe on the lower pedal with your knee nearly straight but not strained.

Fig. 5.4 Seat height determination

Sit on the bike and place your heels on the pedals. In case you have pedals with toeclips they must be turned upside down. Pedal backwards this way, making sure you do not have to rock from side to side to reach the pedals. Now lower the saddle by whatever is the difference in height between heels and soles. Tighten the saddle in this position. Note that the heels-on-pedals style only applies

or straighten his arms to get lower or higher. This may be required to apply more force to the pedals or to reduce the wind resistance by lowering the front, or to get a better view by raising the front a little.

## Saddle Height

The height of the saddle, or rather the distance of its top relative to the pedals, is the most critical variable for effective cycling. Though it is varied to when adjusting the seat height, not to riding the bike. When cycling, the ball of the foot (the second joint of the big toe) should be over the center of the pedal axle, with the heel raised so that the knee is never fully straightened.

You may have to do some fine-tuning to achieve long-term comfort. Riders with disproportionately small feet may want to place the saddle a little lower, those with big feet perhaps slightly higher. No need to get carried away: raise or lower the seat in steps of 6 mm (¼ in) at a time and try to get used to any position by riding several hundred miles or several days before attempting any change, which again must be about 6 mm to make any real difference.

Fig. 5.5 Knee over pedal center

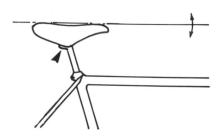

Fig. 5.6 Saddle angle

### Saddle Position and Angle

The normal saddle position is such that the seat post is roughly in the middle of the saddle. For optimum pedalling efficiency, adjust the saddle forward or backwards after it has been set to the correct height. On any regular mountain bike, sitting on the bike with the front of the foot on the pedal and the crank placed horizontally, the center of the knee joint should be vertically aligned with the spindle of the forward pedal, as shown in Fig. 5.5. You can locate the center of the knee joint at the bony protrusion just behind the knee cap.

The angle of the saddle relative to the horizontal plane should initially be set so as to keep the line that connects the highest points at the front and the back level, as illustrated in Fig. 5.6. It may be necessary to modify this angle to prevent slipping forward or backwards once the handlebars have been set to the correct height. This may not become apparent until after some miles of cycling. Adjusting procedures for both forward position and angle are outlined below.

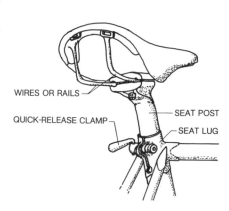

WIRES OR RAILS

QUICK-RELEASE CLAMP

SEAT POST

SEAT LUG

Fig. 5.7 Saddle adjustments

### Saddle Adjustments

To carry out the actual mechanical adjustment on the saddle, first take a close look at the way it is installed on the bike, comparing it with Fig. 5.7. The saddle height is easy to adjust on a mountain bike. Loosen the quick-release binder bolt behind the seat lug; raise or lower the saddle with the attached seat post in a twisting motion, and tighten the binder bolt again when the saddle is at the right height, making sure it is straight.

If your bike is equipped with a height adjusting spring device, such as the Hite-Rite, you will be able to adjust the seat within an adequate range very conveniently. Just apply the right amount of downward force to let the spring adjuster raise or lower the seat to the desired position. If the presently set range should be exceeded, which is rarely the case but may occur when adjusting a bike for a different rider or when it is first installed, refer to Chapter 17 for the appropriate instructions.

To change the saddle's forward position, undo the adjustment bolts (only one bolt on some models) on your seat post. These bolts are usually reached from under the saddle cover, though they may be accessible instead from below or the side on some models. Some older mountain bike seat posts also have a quick-release here. Once loosened, push the saddle forward or backward until the desired position is reached, then tighten the bolts, making sure the saddle is held under the desired angle relative to the horizontal plane.

**Handlebar Height and Position**

Even on a mountain bike, the highest point of the handlebars should be lower than the top of the saddle to ride efficiently. Just how low will be determined by the shape of the handlebars and the rider's physiognomy. This depends on the relative distribution of body weight and height, as well as the upper and lower arm length. Only by experimenting can a rider determine what will work best for him. Here I shall simply tell you how to determine the initial position for a frame size

check, followed by the adjustment for a relaxed initial riding style. You should developed enough sensitivity to fine-tune the handlebar height and stem length to match your needs perfectly after about a thousand miles of cycling.

To set the handlebars for a relaxed riding posture, proceed as follows. First set the top of the bars about 3 cm (1 1/4 in) lower than the saddle. Sit on the bike and reach forward for the handgrips, as though ready to grab the brake handles. In this position your shoulders should be about midway between seat and hands, as shown in Fig. 5.3 at the beginning of this chapter. The arms should feel neither stretched nor heavily loaded and should not project sideways from the shoulder width too much.

If your hands are much further apart than the shoulders, the handlebars are too wide. They can either be replaced or cut off at the ends. I have never yet seen the opposite phenomenon on any mountain bike, namely that the handlebars were too narrow. If you can not find a relaxed position, you may need a longer or shorter stem. You may have to twist the handlebars a little in the stem, to find the most comfortable position; the latter adjustment is also outlined below.

If you should have a particularly short combination of lower arms and torso in relation to your leg length, you may not be comfortable even with a short stem. In that case, a smaller frame, which generally also has a shorter top tube, may be in order — with an overlong seatpost installed. If no bike can be found with the right top tube length, you may need a custom-built frame with the desired dimensions of seat tube and top tube. This would be the ultimate solution, although it is probably not so critical that you can't make do with a stock frame.

## Handlebar Adjustments

You are referred to the accompanying illustration Fig. 5.8. To vary the height of the handlebars, straddle the front wheel, clamping it between your legs. Undo the expander bolt, which is recessed in the top of the stem. If the stem does not come loose immediately, you may have to lift the handlebars to raise the wheel off the ground, then tap on the head of the expander bolt with a hammer. This will loosen the internal clamping device. Now raise or lower the handlebar stem as required. Tighten the expander bolt again, while holding the handlebars straight in the desired position.

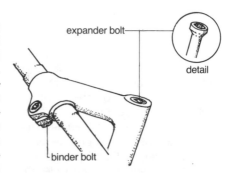

Fig. 5.8 Handlebar adjustments

To change the angle of the handlebar ends with respect to the horizontal plane, undo the binder bolt that clamps the handlebar bend in the front of the stem. Twist the handlebar bend until it is under the desired angle, and then tighten the binder bolt again, holding the bar centered. Older mountain bikes may have a stem with a V-shaped reach, equipped with two or even four binder bolts holding the handlebars. To install a longer stem or a different bar design, you are referred to the instructions in Chapter 16 or to your friendly bike store.

The correct handlebar position often puts more strain on the hands than beginning cyclists find comfortable, especially when rough surfaces cause vibrations. Minimize this problem by keeping the arms slightly bent, never holding them in a cramped position. If you still experience discomfort, get cushioned foam handgrips, rather than firm plastic grips, if the latter are installed on your bike. Wearing gloves will also release the strain.

Once you start riding off-road, especially in mountainous terrain, you may want to lower the saddle or move it further back to cycle down a steep incline. Since the variations in geometry from one make and model to the next are quite significant, you may have to do a bit of experimenting to find the best positions for such special uses.

## Getting on and off

Once saddle and handlebars are adjusted correctly, it will be time to start riding your bike. In case you are not yet familiar with the bicycle, here's a suggestion for getting on and off the bike. All other riding and handling techniques involve prolonged learning processes that will be treated in Part II. However, the simple act of starting the bike should be mastered immediately. Easy though this may seem, it is worth practicing, if only to avoid embarrassing or dangerous mishaps, especially when cycling with others or in traffic. You will learn more advanced methods, appropriate to regular and specific off-road riding practice, respectively, in Chapters 7 and 8.

Since even mountain bikes are ridden on regular roads where there is traffic to worry about much of the time, I shall include references to your safety involving considerations for other vehicles. To some extent, these apply on the trail as well, where you may get in the way of other trail users, including other bicyclists. Of course, most cyclists are not entirely new to the game: you too may feel you've been cycling long enough to do without any additional advice or practice. It still does not hurt to follow the procedures described below. Do it consciously, so you become more efficient at handling the bike when cycling off-road as well.

Before starting off, make sure your shoe laces are tied and tucked in, or are short enough not to run the risk of getting caught in the chain. Select a low gear, with the chain on the middle chainwheel and an intermediate or big sprocket. Start off at the side of the road, after having checked to make sure no traffic is following closely behind. Straddle the top tube by swinging the appropriate leg either over the handlebars, the top tube, or the saddle. Hold the handlebars with both hands and place one foot on the corresponding pedal, the other on the ground.

Look behind you to make sure the road is clear, then check ahead to establish which course you want to follow. Place your weight on the pedal, leaning lightly on the handlebars, and start forward. Put the other foot on the other pedal when it is in the top position.

To slow down, whether just to stop or to get off the bike, look behind you, to make sure you are not getting in the way of following cyclists or motorists. Aim for the place where you want to stop. Change into a lower gear, appropriate for starting off again later. Slow down by braking gently, using mainly the front brake to stop. Just before you have come to a standstill, lean in the direction you want to dismount. Place the foot on the ground, while moving forward off the saddle to straddle the seat tube. Now you are in the right position to dismount or start again.

If you want to get off the bike at this point, lift the other leg over, balancing away from the bike. However, under most circumstances, especially when loaded with luggage, you will find that the machine is most easily controlled when you remain on the bike, straddling the top tube. Consequently, I suggest you only dismount completely if it is really necessary.

# Part II
# Getting the Most out of Your Mountain Bike

Downhill artist Everett
Utterbach coming down
fast. (Photo Donald
Favello)

# 6
# Understanding and Using the Gears

All mountain bikes are equipped with a sophisticated derailleur system for multiple gearing. To change gear, the chain is shifted onto another combination of chainwheel and sprocket with the aid of two derailleur mechanisms. On these machines fifteen and eighteen speed systems are generally used, though ten-speed or twelve-speed gearing may be adequate for some applications. On the latter, two chainwheels are used in combination with five or six sprockets, respectively. The more common fifteen and eighteen speed systems have three chainwheels, again combined with five or six sprockets, respectively.

The derailleur method of gearing allows minute adjustments of the gear ratio to the cyclist's potential on the one hand, and the terrain, wind resistance and surface conditions on the other. All this is mere theory for most riders, because the majority of people, including most beginning mountain bike riders, plod along in the wrong gear for the work load. Indeed, learning to select the right gear may well provide the biggest single step towards improved cycling speed and endurance. That's the subject of the present chapter.

There is a sound theory behind the principle of gear selection, based on the optimum pedalling rate, which I have covered in several of my other books, such as the *Bicycle Racing Guide*. Interesting though this theory is, one need not wait to apply the technique until it is thoroughly understood. That's why I shall limit the background information here to what you should know to select your gears correctly.

### The Derailleur System

Fig. 6.1 shows and names the mechanical components of the derailleur system as used on the mountain bike. The chain runs over (usually) three chainrings, also referred to as chainwheels, which are mounted on the RH crank, and any one of five or six sprockets mounted on a freewheel block at the rear wheel. As long as you

Fig. 6.1 The derailleur system

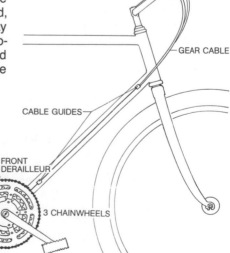

THUMB SHIFTERS

GEAR CABLE

CABLE GUIDES

FREEWHEEL WITH SPROCKETS

FRONT DERAILLEUR

REAR DERAILLEUR

3 CHAINWHEELS

are pedalling forward, the chain can be moved from one chainwheel to the other by means of the front derailleur or changer, and from one sprocket to another by means of the rear derailleur. Systems with seven sprockets are also available, but are not generally considered suitable for mountain bike use, since these offset the rear wheel too much.

The various chainwheels and sprockets have different numbers of teeth. Consequently, the ratio between pedalling speed and the speed with which the rear wheel is driven changes whenever a different combination is selected. As illustrated in Fig. 6.2, bigger chainrings in the front and smaller sprockets in the rear result in higher gears, whereas smaller chainrings and bigger sprockets give lower gears. Higher gears are selected when the cycling is easy, so the available output allows a high riding speed. Select a lower gear when higher resistances must be overcome, such as riding uphill or against a head wind, or when starting off from a standstill.

On the mountain bike, each derailleur is controlled by means of a shift lever that is mounted on the handlebars, within easy reach without taking the hands off the grips. A typical thumb shifter is shown in Fig. 6.3.

Most shifts are made with the rear derailleur, while the front changer is primarily used to move from one general range of gears to the other. With the usual fifteen or eighteen speed set-up, all the gears in the high range are reached by shifting the rear derailleur, while the front derailleur remains on the largest chainring. The intermediate gears are reached while the front derailleur is set to engage the intermediate chainring. All the gears in the low range are selected with the front changer in the position to put the chain on the smallest chainring.

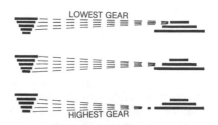

Fig. 6.2 Gear determined by sprocket and chainwheel size

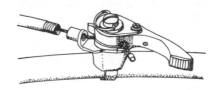

Fig. 6.3 Thumb shifter

Though it is possible to select chainwheel and sprocket sizes in such a way that intermediate gears between rear derailleur shifts are always reached with a front changer shift, the above method simplifies the gear selection procedure considerably. This is certainly so for the typical mountain bike set-up with fifteen or eighteen speed gearing, where you often have to change quickly under difficult conditions.

The rear derailleur is controlled by means of the RH shifter. To put the chain on a different sprocket in the rear, move the RH shift lever, while pedalling forward with reduced force. Pull the lever back to change to a larger sprocket, which results in a lower gear; push it forward to reach a smaller sprocket, resulting in a higher gear. Nowadays, virtually all rear derailleurs are indexed, meaning that they always move in distinct steps from one sprocket to the next. Older models may not be indexed, and – believe it or not – one can learn to shift these delicate devices just as accurately: it just takes more practice and sensitivity.

The LH shift lever controls the front derailleur or changer, which simply shoves the cage through which the chain runs to the right or the left, placing the chain onto a larger or smaller chainwheel, respectively. Pulling the lever back engages a larger chainwheel for a higher gear range on most models; pushing it forward engages a smaller chainwheel, obtaining a lower gearing range.

### Gearing Theory

Gearing enables you to pedal at an efficient rate with comfortable force under a wide range of conditions and riding speeds. If the combination of chainwheel and sprocket size were fixed, as it is on the single-speed bicycle, any given pedalling speed would invariably correspond to a certain riding speed. The rear wheel would be turning at a speed that can be simply calculated by multiplying the pedalling rate with the quotient of chainwheel and sprocket sizes (expressed in terms of their respective numbers of teeth):

$$V_{wheel} = V_{pedal} \times T_{front} / T_{rear}$$

where:
$V_{wheel}$ = wheel rotating speed (RPM)
$V_{pedal}$ = pedalling rate (RPM)
$T_{front}$ = number of teeth, chainwheel
$T_{rear}$ = number of teeth, sprocket

The actual riding speed depends on this wheel rotating speed and the effective wheel diameter. The effective diameter of a nominal 26 inch wheel is about 650 mm. This results in a riding speed in MPH that can be determined by multiplying the wheel speed in RPM by 0.075. These two calculations can be combined to find the riding speed in MPH directly from the pedalling rate and the chainwheel and sprocket sizes as follows:

$$MPH = 0.075 \times V_{pedal} \times T_{front} / T_{rear}$$

where:
MPH = riding speed in MPH and the other symbols are as defined above. To express riding speed in km/h, use the following formula instead:

$$km/h = 0.12 \times V_{pedal} \times T_{front} / T_{rear}$$

To give an example, assume you are pedalling at a rate of 80 RPM on a bike geared with a 42 tooth chainwheel and a 21 tooth rear sprocket. Your riding speed, expressed in MPH and km/h respectively, will be:

$$0.075 \times 80 \times 42 / 21 = 12 \text{ MPH}$$

$$0.12 \times 80 \times 42 / 21 = 19 \text{ km/h}$$

Depending on the prevailing terrain conditions, this may be too easy or too hard for optimum endurance perfor-

This is what happens when you change gear with the rear derailleur: the chain is simply shoved over sideways to a bigger or smaller sprocket.

mance. If you are riding up a steep incline, this speed may require a very high pedal force, which may be too exhausting and damaging to muscles, joints and tendons. On a level road the same speed will be reached so easily that you don't feel any significant resistance.

The derailleur gearing system allows you to choose the combination of chainwheel and sprocket sizes that enables you to operate effectively at your chosen pedalling speed with optimum performance. You may of course also vary the pedalling rate, which would appear to have the same effect as selecting another gear. Indeed, with any given gear, pedalling slower reduces riding speed and therefore demands less power, whereas a higher pedalling rate increases road speed, requiring more power.

However, power output is not the sole, nor indeed the most important, criterion. Performing at a given power output may tax the body differently, depending on the associated force and speed of movement. It has been found that to cycle long distances effectively, without tiring or hurting excessively, the pedal force must be kept down by pedalling at a rate well above what seems natural to the beginning cyclist.

Whereas the beginner tends to plod along at 40–60 RPM, efficient long duration cycling requires a pedalling rate of 80 RPM or more. Racers generally pedal even faster, whether riding off-road or not. This skill doesn't come overnight, the cyclist first has to learn to move his legs that fast, but it is an essential requirement for efficient bicycling. Much of your early cycling practice should therefore be aimed at mastering the art of fast pedalling, referred to as *spinning*.

## Gearing Practice

Once you know that high gears mean big chainwheels and small sprockets, it's time to get some practice riding in high and low gears. First do it 'dry': the bike upside down or supported with the rear wheel off the ground. Turn the cranks by hand and use the shift levers to change up and down, front and rear, until you have developed a good idea of the combinations reached in all conceivable shift lever positions.

Listen for rubbing and crunching noises as you shift, realizing that the shift has not been executed properly until the noises have subdued. Generally, noises come from the front, since the indexing takes care of such problems in the rear. You may have to move the shifter for the front derailleur if you discern a noise after a rear derailleur shift, since the chain – now running under a different angle – may be rubbing against the front derailleur.

Now take to the road or any other level terrain. Select a place where you can experiment with your gears without the risk of being run over by a closely following vehicle or getting in the way of other cyclists. Start off in a low gear and shift the rear derailleur up in steps. Then shift to another chainwheel and change down through the gears with the rear derailleur, followed by the same changes with the chain on the third chainwheel.

When shifting, reduce the pedal force, still pedalling forward. The front derailleur in particular will not shift as smoothly as it did when the cranks were turned by hand. You will notice that the noises become more severe and that shifts don't take place as you intended. To execute a correct front change, you may have to overshift slightly first: push the lever a little beyond the correct position to affect a definite change, then back up until the chain is quiet again. Practice shifting until it goes smoothly.

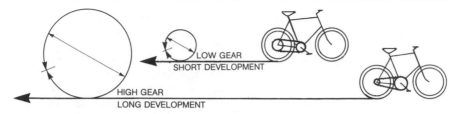

Fig. 6.4 Gear and development

All this can be learned if you give it time and attention. Some people never learn, quite simply because they don't take the trouble to practice conscientiously. Others take that trouble and learn to shift predictably and smoothly within a week. All it takes to become an expert very quickly, is half an hour of intensive practice each day during one week, and the continued attention required to do it right during regular riding afterwards.

### Gear Designation

Just how high or low any given gear is, may be expressed by giving the respective chainwheel and · sprocket size engaged in the particular gear. However, this is not a very good measure. It may not be immediately clear that a combination designated 42 X 16 has the same effect as one designated 52 X 21, though they really do result in the same ratio, as can be verified mathematically. It will become clear that it is nearly impossible to compare gears this way on bikes with different wheel sizes.

To allow a direct comparison between the gearing effects of different gears and bikes, two methods are in use, referred to as gear number and development, respectively, as illustrated in Fig. 6.4. The gear number is determined by multiplying the quotient of chainwheel and sprocket sizes with the wheel diameter in inches:

$$gear = D_{wheel} \times T_{front} / T_{rear}$$

where:
gear = gear number in inches
$D_{wheel}$ = wheel diameter in inches
$T_{front}$ = number of teeth, chainwheel
$T_{rear}$ = number of teeth, sprocket

Returning to the example of a bike with 26 inch wheels, geared with a 42 tooth chainwheel and a 21 tooth sprocket, the gear number would be:

$$26 \times 42 / 21 = 52 \text{ in}$$

This is the customary, though rather quaint, method used in the English speaking world to define bicycle gearing. The rest of the world expresses gears in terms of *development*. This is the distance in meters covered by the bike with one crank revolution. Development is calculated as follows:

$$Dev. = 3.14 \times d_{wheel} \times T_{front} / T_{rear}$$

where:
Dev. = development in meters
$d_{wheel}$ = wheel size in m
$T_{front}$ = number of teeth, chainwheel
$T_{rear}$ = number of teeth, sprocket

The development for the same example would be:

$$3.14 \times 0.650 \times 42 / 21 = 4.10 \text{ m}$$

In practice, you are not expected to figure this out yourself. Instead, you may refer to the tables in the Appendix. Just remember that a high gear is expressed by a high gear number or a long development. For off-road purposes, gear ranges tend to be lower than they are on other bikes. Low gears in terms of gear number are in the low to mid twenties (around 1.90–2.20 m in terms of development). The highest gears are those above 80 in (development of more than 6.40 m).

## Gear Selection

Possibly the biggest problem for the beginning cyclist is to select the right gear out of the bewildering array available. To generalize, I would say it's whichever gear allows you to maximize your pedalling rate without diminishing your capacity to work effectively.

Perhaps you are initially able to pedal no faster than 60 RPM. That'll be too low once you have had some riding practice, but for now that may be your limit. So the right gear is the one in which you can reach that rate at any time, preferably exceeding it. Count it out with the aid of a wrist watch until you develop a feel for your pedalling speed. If you find yourself pedalling slower, change down into a slightly lower gear to increase the pedalling rate at the same riding speed. If you're pedalling faster, keep it up until you feel you are indeed spinning too lightly, and then change to a slightly higher gear to increase road speed at the same pedalling rate.

Gradually, you will develop the capacity to pedal faster. As this happens, increase the pedalling rate along with your ability, moving up from 60 to 70, 80 and eventually even higher. When riding with others, don't be guided by their gear selection, since they may be stronger or weaker, or may have developed their pedalling speed more or less than you have.

It should not take long before you can judge the right gear in advance, without the need to count out the pedal revolutions. You know when to change down into a lower gear as the direction of the road changes, exposing you to a head wind, or when you reach an incline. You will also learn to judge just how far to change down – and up again when the conditions become more favorable. Change gears consciously and frequently in small steps, and you will soon master the trick.

## Derailleur Care and Adjustment

For optimum operation of the derailleur system, several things should be regularly checked and corrected if necessary. The derailleurs themselves, as well as the chain and the various sprockets, chainwheels and control cables, must be kept clean and lightly lubricated. Cables for index shifting systems should be kept clean, but not lubricated. The cables must be just taut when the shift levers are pushed forward and the derailleurs engage the appropriate gear. The tension screws on the shift levers must be kept tightened to give positive shifting without excessive tightness or slack.

When the chain is shifted beyond the biggest or smallest chainwheel or sprocket, or when certain combinations can not be reached, the derailleurs themselves must be adjusted. They are equipped with set-stop screws, which can be adjusted with a small screwdriver. Instructions for this and all other derailleur maintenance work can be found in Chapter 19.

# 7
# Bike Handling Skills

Basically, riding a mountain bike is like riding any other bike – only more so. The combination of rough surfaces and high downhill speeds may prove tricky if you are not properly prepared. On the other hand, you have the right machine to do some things easily that would otherwise be difficult. To competently and confidently ride off-road, you have to be in complete command of your machine. In this chapter and the one that follows, we will take a closer look at these skills, and you will be shown how to achieve the necessary mastery.

The present chapter deals with increasing your basic competence at handling the beast, with proper control over the steering and braking mechanisms. This will help you cycle with minimal effort and maximum confidence, whether on the road or off-road. In the next chapter, you will be

Frog-eye view of a mountain bike being launched at a rough place. (James Cassimus photograph)

introduced to the peculiarities of effective riding techniques that are specific to off-road use. Although an understanding of the theoretical background is helpful, I shall concentrate as much as possible on the practical aspects, telling you how to practice what you learn.

### The Steering Principle
The bicycle is not steered most effectively by merely turning the handlebars and following the front wheel, as is the case for any two-track vehicle, such as a car. Though bicycles and other single-track vehicles indeed follow the front wheel, they also require the rider to lean his vehicle into the curve to balance it at the same time, so it doesn't topple over to the outside of the curve due to the centrifugal force.

If you were to merely turn the handlebars, the lower part of the bike would start running away from its previous course in the direction which the

front wheel is pointed. Meanwhile, the mass of the rider, perched high up on the bike, would continue following the original course due to inertia. Thus, the center of gravity would not be in line with the supporting bike, and the rider would come crashing to the ground. Due to the effect of centrifugal force, the tendency to throw the rider off towards the outside of the curve increases with higher speeds, requiring a more pronounced lean into the curve the faster you are going.

It is possible to steer by turning the handlebars, and then correct lean and steering to regain balance afterwards. In fact, many older people, especially women, seem to do it that way, succeeding quite well at low speeds. As soon as imbalance becomes imminent, they have to make a correction in the other direction. After some more cramped and anxious movements, they finally get around the corner. This accounts for the tense and impulsive riding style typical of such riders. They have ridden this way so long that they don't realize their movements are awkward and their balance is precarious.

The more effective technique for riding a curve at speed is to place the bike under the appropriate angle, where the centrifugal force is offset by a shift of your weight to the inside, before turning. Two methods may be used, depending on the amount of time and room available to carry out the maneuver. I refer to these two methods as the natural and the forced turn, respectively. To understand either, we should first take a look at the intricacies of balancing the bike when riding a straight line, after which the two methods of turning can be explained.

### Bicycle Balance

What keeps a bicycle or any other single track vehicle going without falling over is the inertia of its moving mass. Rolling a narrow hoop, such as a bicycle rim, will show that it has an unstable balance: once the thing starts to lean either left or right, it will go further and further down, until it hits the ground. This is because the mass is no longer supported vertically in line with the force. Try it with a bicycle wheel if you like. If the bike's front wheel could not be steered and the rider couldn't move sideways, he'd very soon come down the same way.

On the bicycle, the rider notices when the vehicle starts to lean over. Theoretically, there are two ways out of the predicament: either move the rider back over the center of the bike, or move the bike back under the rider. In practice, the latter method is used most effectively, especially at higher speeds. When the bike begins leaning to the side, the rider oversteers the front wheel a little in the same direction, which restores the balance. In fact, this point will be passed, so the bike starts leaning the other way, and so on.

This entire sequence of movements is easy to notice when you are cycling slowly. When standing still, the balancing motions are so extreme that only a highly skilled cyclist can keep control. The faster the bicycle, the less perceptible (though equally important and therefore harder to master) are the steering corrections required to retain balance. To get an understanding of this whole process, I suggest you practice riding a straight line at a low speed. Then do it at a higher speed, and see whether you agree with the explanation, referring also to Fig. 7.1.

Clearly, both riding a straight line and staying upright with the bike are merely illusions. In reality, the bike is always in disequilibrium, following a more or less curved track. Bike and rider lean alternately one way or the

Lean in the direction of the turn. At higher speeds a more pronounced lean is necessary to induce the same curve. At any speed a tighter curve requires more lean.

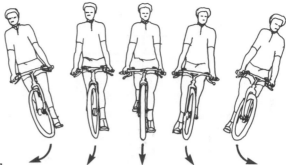

Fig. 7.1 Bike lean and steering

other. At higher speeds the curves are longer and gentler, while the amount of lean can be perceptible; at lower speeds the curves are shorter and sharper, with a less pronounced lean angle for any given deviation.

### The Natural Turn

Under normal circumstances, the rider knows well ahead of time where to turn, and there is enough room to follow a wide curve. This is the situation in a natural turn, illustrated in Fig. 7.2. It makes use of the lean that results from normal straight path steering corrections. To turn to the right, you simply wait until the bike is leaning that way, while the left turn is initiated when the bike is leaning to the left.

Instead of turning the handlebars to that same side, as you would do to get back in balance riding straight, you leave the handlebars alone. This causes the bike to lean further and further in the direction of the turn. Only when the lean is quite significant, do you steer in the same direction, but not as abruptly as you would to straighten up. Instead, you fine-tune the ratio of lean and steering to ride the curve out.

You will still be leaning in the same direction when the turn is completed, and you would ride a circle without some corrective action on your part. You get back on a straight course by

steering further into the curve than the amount of lean demands to maintain your balance. This allows you to resume the slightly curving course with which you approximate the straight line.

Unconsciously, you probably learned to do this when you were a kid, but never realized what was going on. You could perhaps continue to ride a bicycle forever without understanding the theory. However, to keep control over the bike in demanding situations encountered while riding off-road, you will be better off if you have the theoretical knowledge and have learned to ride a calculated course, making use of this information. Get a feel for it by riding around an empty parking lot or any other level area many times, leaning this way and that, following straight lines and making turns, until it is second nature and something you can do consciously.

While you are practicing this technique, as well as when riding at other times, note that speed, curve radius and lean are all closely correlated. A sharper turn requires more lean at any given speed. At a higher speed, any given curve requires greater lean angles than the same curve radius at a lower speed. As you practice this technique, learn to judge which are the appropriate combinations and limitations under different circumstances.

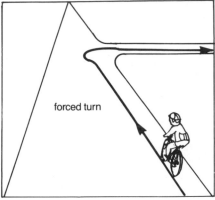

Fig. 7.2 The natural turn

Fig. 7.3 The forced turn

### The Forced Turn

Especially off road, you will often be confronted with situations in which you can't wait until you are leaning the right way to make a natural turn. Ir-regularities in the surface, the presence of obstacles or the presence of other trail users may force you into a narrow predetermined path, with only a few inches to spare. Or you may have to get around a curve that is too sharp to be taken naturally at your current riding speed.

These situations require the second method of turning, which I call the forced turn, illustrated in Fig. 7.3. In this case, the turn must be initiated quickly, regardless of which way the bike happens to be leaning. You have to coerce the bike to lean in the appropriate direction and at an adequate angle just at the right time. And it has to be done quickly.

Do that by sharply steering *away* from the turn just before you get there. You and the bike will immediately start to lean in the direction of the turn. You risk a disastrous crash, as your bike moves away from the mass center, if you continue in a straight line. You have quickly achieved a considerable lean angle in the direction of the turn. Compensate for this by steering abruptly in the same direction. Since this

is the direction of the turn, you are set up just right to make a sharp turn. Once completed, steer into the turn a little further, to regain the approximately straight course, as explained for the natural turn.

The forced turn technique must be practiced intensely and consciously, since it by no means comes naturally. The beginning cyclists has to overcome all sorts of reasonable inhibitions and practice a lot before he can initiate a *left* turn by steering *right*. Take your bike to a level, grassy area or an empty parking lot a few days in a row, wearing protective clothing in case you fall: helmet, gloves, jacket and long pants.

Practice and experiment until you've mastered the trick, and refresh your skill from time to time, until this instant turning technique has become second nature. Figures 7.2 and 7.3 compare the paths taken in the natural and the forced turn, respectively. The latter will be helpful when making a tight turn, and is of equal benefit when you need to temporarily divert from your straight course for some reason. In Chapter 8, you will be shown how to apply it to the difficult task of avoiding a suddenly emerging obstacle.

### Braking Technique

The mountain bike rider often has to use the brakes, though not always to make a panic stop. In fact, the sensible cyclist should hardly ever have to brake to a standstill. Instead, he will use the brakes to control and regulate his speed. Effective braking means that you can ride up fast close to the turn or the obstacle that requires the reduced speed, brake to reach the lower speed quickly, and accelerate immediately afterwards.

You will be using the brakes to get down in speed from 30 to 20 MPH to take a turn, or from 30 to 28 MPH to avoid running into the person ahead of you. Or you may have to get down from 50 to 10 MPH to handle a switchback or avoid a tree or rock on a steep descent. To do this effectively without risk requires an understanding of braking physics. Though at times you may have to reduce your speed quickly, you should also develop a feel for gradual speed reduction to prevent skidding and loss of control. In fact, most cyclists are more often in danger due to braking too vigorously than due to insufficient stopping power.

Applying the brakes results in deceleration or speed reduction, which can only take place more or less gradually. The rate of deceleration can be measured and is expressed in $m/sec^2$. A deceleration of $1 \, m/sec^2$ means that after each second of braking the travelling speed is $1 \, m/sec$ less than it was at the beginning of that second. A speed of 30 MPH corresponds to $13 \, m/sec$. Getting down to standstill would take 13 sec if the deceleration is $1 \, m/sec^2$; it would take 4 seconds to reach $9 \, m/sec$ or 20 MPH. At a higher rate of deceleration it would take less time (and a shorter distance) to get down to the desired speed.

The modern mountain bike has remarkably effective brakes, providing it's not raining. A modest force on the brake handle can cause a deceleration of $4-5 \, m/sec^2$ with just one brake. Applying both brakes, the effect is even more dramatic, enabling you to slow down from 30 to 15 MPH within one second. There are some limitations to braking that have to be considered though.

In the first place, moisture has a negative effect on the rim brake's performance, as the build-up of water on the rims reduces the friction between brake block and rim drastically. This applies especially if ordinary rubber brake blocks are used. With any rubber brake blocks, I measured a reduc-

Downhill braking on rough ground has to be practiced. Keep the speed under control before you get going so fast that drastic deceleration would be needed.

tion from 4.5 to 1.5 m/sec$^2$ for a given hand lever force and half that figure for bicycles with chrome plated steel rims. These should therefore not be used on any bike with rim brakes. Lately, special brake block materials have .been introduced that are less sensitive to rain, but I am still waiting for the superior material used for the Modolo D-1000 racing brake blocks to become available in a version to match the typical mountain bike brake.

The second limitation is associated with a change in the distribution of weight between the wheels as a result of braking. Because the mass center of the rider is quite high above the road, and its horizontal distance to the front wheel axle comparatively small, the bicycle has a tendency to tip forward in response to deceleration. Weight is transferred from the rear to the front of the bike, as illustrated in Fig. 7.4. When the deceleration reaches about 3.5 m/sec$^2$, the weight on the rear wheel is no longer enough to provide traction. Braking harder than that with the rear brake makes the rear wheel skid, resulting in loss of control.

In a typical riding posture, the rear wheel is unloaded so far the bike actually starts to tip forward when a deceleration of about 6.5 m/sec$^2$ is reached. Consequently, no conventional bicycle can ever be controlled when trying to brake harder than this, regardless of the type, number and quality of the brakes used. This is a very high deceleration, which you should not often reach, but it is good to realize there is such a limit and that it can not be avoided by using the rear brake alone or in addition to the front brake, but only by braking less vigorously. During a sudden speed reduction or panic stop such high deceleration may be reached. On a downslope the effect will be even more pro-

Fig. 7.4 Weight transfer when braking

nounced, since it raises the rider even higher relative to the front wheel. In all such cases, reduce the toppling-over effect by shifting your body weight back and down as much as possible: sit far back and hold the upper body horizontally.

Since twice as great a deceleration is possible with the front brake as with the rear, the former should be used under most conditions. In most circumstances, short of a panic stop, you can brake very effectively by using the front brake alone. When both brakes are used simultaneously, the one in the front can be applied quite a bit harder than the one in the rear. If you notice the rear brake is less effective when pressed equally far, it will be time to check it, and if necessary adjust, lubricate or replace the brake cable.

All the above is fine as long as you are riding a more or less straight line. When riding off-road, you may have to brake in a curve. Under these conditions, all my smart advice about using the front brake may be of little use: since the bike will not be directly in line with the path of travel, it will slip sideways when you apply the brake in a curve. Consequently, distinguish strictly between straight line and curved path braking. In the latter case, use mainly the rear brake.

Better yet, try to brake before you get to the curve, using primarily the front brake.

Most braking is not done abruptly. Gradual braking must also be practiced. Gradual deceleration, particularly when the road is slick, in curves or when others are following closely behind, is vitally important. You must be able to control the braking force within narrow limits. Practice all the various forms and conditions of braking. Pay the utmost attention to the complex relationship between initial speed, curve radius, brake lever force and deceleration, to become fully competent at handling the bike when slowing down under all conceivable circumstances.

On a steep downhill, the slope not only increases the tendency to tip you forward, it also induces an accelerating effect, which must be overcome by the brakes merely to keep the speed constant. A 20 % slope, which is not a rare phenomenon off-road, results in an acceleration of about $2$ m/sec$^2$. Obviously, you will encounter big problems in wet weather on such a downhill stretch if you don't keep your speed down from the start. Reduce the speed by gradual, intermittent braking. This will help wipe most of the water from the rims, retaining braking efficiency a little better. This way, the brakes are not overtaxed when you do have to reduce the speed suddenly, as may be required to handle an unexpected obstacle or a sharp turn.

Effective braking must be practiced to achieve complete control of the bicycle under normal and difficult cycling conditions. The dramatic difference between the bike's behavior when braking on the straight and in a curve must be experienced to be appreciated. Again, this is a matter for practice in a place without traffic. Include braking in your regular exercises during the first weeks of cycling

David Fisher climbing in a two-foot gear at the Shell Ridge Open Space in Wallnut Creek, California. (Photo Donald Favello)

preparation. Even after you have been riding for some time, you will be well advised to repeat from time to time the practice sessions for steering and braking control.

### Other Riding Techniques

Riding a mountain bike with total confidence requires hands-on experience. Most of the associated skills can be learned faster and more thoroughly when you understand the principles that are applied. Building up on the information about posture, gearing, steering and braking provided in the preceding sections, you will be shown here what to do under various typical riding situations. The many miles of experience will come soon enough when you start riding. However, the handling practice is gained more effectively when applying these techniques.

### Getting up to Speed

Though you may not be into cycling for speed alone, you should learn to reach an acceptable speed quickly. You have already been shown how to get on the bike and start off smoothly. The next trick is to reach the ultimate riding speed quickly and efficiently. The idea is to waste as little time and energy as possible during this process of getting up to speed. Tricky, because acceleration demands disproportionately high levels of power output. And the faster it's done, the more demanding it is.

Clearly, you have to strike a balance. Accelerating faster than necessary wastes energy that will be sorely needed later. Done too slowly, it may become a plodding affair, especially if your speed remains inadequate to overcome steep sections or soft ground. You will have to find the right balance between speed and effort, but the way to reach it is easy to describe: start in a low gear and increase speed gradually but rapidly.

There are two methods: either pedal faster and faster in the low gear, changing up only as you reach a significant speed, or be prepared for a surge of hard work, standing on the pedals, throwing your weight from one side to the other. As soon as speed is reached, sit on the saddle and select a good gear for spinning at a comfortable but high pedalling rate. Once you are going at the desired speed, try to maintain it constantly, to save you the effort of accelerating after every slow-down.

### Accelerating

However efficient a constant speed may be, sometimes you want to accelerate to a higher speed. This may be necessary to catch up with other riders, or to avoid getting left behind. In traffic, you may have to accelerate to get across an intersection before the light changes, to avoid running into another vehicle on the road, or to escape a pursuing dog without a leash.

As for getting up to speed in the first place, it is most efficient to increase the speed as gradually as possible. Unless you are already spinning at your highest possible rate, you will find accelerating by increasing pedalling speed more effective than by increasing pedal force in a higher gear. In other words, as long as you can spin faster, it is best to shift down into a slightly lower gear and increase the pedalling rate vigorously. Once you gather momentum and are approaching your maximum spinning speed, shift up and continue to gain speed in the slightly higher gear.

### Riding Against the Wind

At higher speeds or whenever there is a strong head wind, the effect of air drag on the power needed to cycle is quite noticeable. This may not always

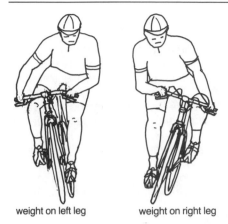

weight on left leg          weight on right leg

Fig. 7.5 Honking, or standing while climbing

versely, using ridiculously low gears when the terrain doesn't call for it. Refer to Chapter 6 for advice on selecting the right gears.

### Climbing Standing up

On extremely steep sections, where even the lowest available gear is too high to allow a smoothly spinning leg motion, it is time to apply another technique. Some riders try to increase the length of the power stroke by means of some hefty ankle twisting, really pushing the leg around. This is

Struggling uphill in a California competitive event (David Epperson/Bicycle Sport photograph)

seem very significant off-road, but certainly when travelling on regular roads and whenever you are in open, level terrain this matters quite a bit. Economize your efforts by minimizing the wind resistance as much as possible. Keep your profile low when cycling against the wind. When riding alone, try to seek out the sheltered parts of the road wherever possible, without exposing yourself to danger.

### Hill Climbing

With some conscious effort, everybody's climbing skills can be improved up to a point, even though some riders are born climbers, while others may have to go uphill slowly all their lives. It is an ability that can be learned and developed well enough by the average rider to handle all the hills he encounters.

A regular pedalling motion is most efficient, and that is best mastered by staying seated in a low gear. Mountain bikes are invariably equipped with gears that are low enough to allow you to get up almost any incline while staying in the saddle. What's lacking is a true understanding of gear selection by many riders. Only too often do I see people plodding up at very low pedalling rates in too high a gear, or conan unnecessarily tiring technique, requiring long muscle work phases and short recovery periods. A better method of high gear, low pedalling speed climbing is referred to as honking in Britain, and seems to be a mystery to most American cyclists.

Honking makes use of the rider's body weight to push down the pedals. The weight of the whole body is pulled up after each stroke very quickly. In this mode, the muscle work is done each time the body is raised, rather than when pushing the pedal down and around. To do it effectively, you can either take quick snappy steps, or throw your weight from side to side in a swinging motion, as illustrated in Fig. 7.5. I suggest you practice honking as well as spinning: the one in a relatively high gear at pedalling speeds below 55 RPM, the other in a considerably lower gear at 65 RPM or more. Avoid pedalling rates of 55–65 RPM by choosing you gears so as to stay within either one range or the other.

Here's the right way to carry your mountain bike: top tube over the shoulder, holding the handlebars with one hand, while keeping the other hand free. (David Epperson/ Bicycle Sport photograph)

# 8
# Off-Road Riding Techniques

This chapter will expand on the material introduced in the preceding chapter to develop specific off-road riding skills. Though the basic techniques are the same, the particular applications and their circumstances are different enough to justify special treatment. Just the same, we'll start with what may seem to be the simplest feat possible, gradually expanding our practice to some of the really gonzo tricks that only experienced off-road cyclists have learned to master.

### The Running Start
Since the mountain bike is tough enough to be handled less gingerly than a fragile racer, you can actually jump on board when mounting. There

Everett Utterbach demonstrating a foot down turn in the Redwood Regional Park. (Photo Donald Favello)

are two good ways to do it: with or without a running start. To mount without a running start, select a low or intermediate gear. Place the left crank in the horizontal forward position, holding the bike by the ends of the handlebars. Place the left foot on the pedal and push off with the other leg swinging it over the saddle before losing momentum. Find the RH pedal and keep pedalling, shifting to a higher gear when you've gained speed. To do a running start, start off in a higher gear, swing your leg over and hop in the saddle.

### Walking the Bike
Though bicycles are meant to be ridden, your mountain bike may occasionally have to be walked or even carried. It may not seem difficult to walk, whether with or without your bike; yet

there is a distinct skill that allows you to do it effectively. In off-road situations, you may have to dismount suddenly to walk or even carry the bike part of the way, over obstacles or through a muddy or sandy patch.

Once you have traversed the difficult section, you should be able to get back on without undue loss of time and energy. Doing this skillfully is particularly important in off-road racing, but can also help you enjoy recreational off-road riding.Calculate ahead of time where you will have to get off and shift down to a low gear. Move forward off the saddle and transfer your weight to the pedal on the side you want to get off – usually the left.

Slow down as appropriate for the situation and swing the free leg over when you get to a modest speed, holding it on the other side of the bike just behind the other leg. Calculate where you are going to stop and slow down to jogging speed when you are ready to dismount. Now swing the free leg through, between the other leg and the bike and take a sizeable step forward, moving away from the bike just enough to avoid the pedal from overtaking you in a painful manner. Keep trotting or slow down to a walking pace, holding the bike either by the handlebar ends or by handlebars and saddle.

Now you can either walk or carry the bike. In case you have to carry it to overcome serious obstacles, let the hand on the far side slide down from the handlebars along the down tube, grabbing it a little below the middle, while still trotting or walking. At this point, raise the bike up on your shoulder, letting it slip into place at the point where seat tube and top tube come together. Installing a padded strap there will help protect your shoulder. Grab the handlebars near the middle with the arm that goes through the frame, keeping the other hand free.

After you have carried the bike over the obstacle, you may either want to walk by the side of the bike or get back on. Either way, lower the bike off the shoulder and grab the handlebars with both ends. To walk the bike, just continue this way. To get back on quickly, keep trotting and remount as described at the beginning of this chapter.

### Avoiding Obstacles

Off-road, you will often be confronted with some kind of obstacle that would be small enough to avoid, if it were not right in your path. This may be anything from a pothole or a broken branch to a crashed cyclist just in front of you. Depending how much time and room you have available, use either the natural or the forced turn technique described in Chapter 8. If there is enough room and time to use the natural turn, do so. Since at speed it is hard to go anywhere except where you are actually looking, don't look at the object but at the point where you want to pass it, steering to do so in a natural way.

To cycle around an obstacle that appears suddenly, you can develop a technique based on the forced turn. This maneuver is illustrated in Fig. 8.1. As soon as you perceive the obstacle ahead of you, decide whether to pass it to the left or the right. Ride straight up to it and then, before you reach it, briefly but decisively steer in the direction *opposite* to the obstacle (to the right if you want to pass it on the left). This makes the bike lean over towards the other side. Now steer in that direction just as quickly, which will result in a very sharp forced turn. As soon as you've passed the obstacle, oversteer a little more, causing a lean that helps put the bike back on its proper course.

These techniques can be practiced on an empty parking lot or any other level area, wearing a helmet and two

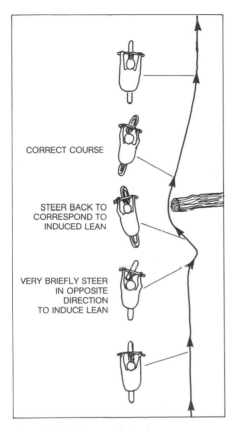

CORRECT COURSE

STEER BACK TO CORRESPOND TO INDUCED LEAN

VERY BRIEFLY STEER IN OPPOSITE DIRECTION TO INDUCE LEAN

Fig. 8.1 Avoiding an obstacle

long sleeved shirts. Mark phoney obstacles with chalk or put down foam pads or sponges. Practice passing them gradually and abruptly on both sides, using the two techniques in turn, until you've mastered the trick. Only then should you try doing the same in more difficult terrain.

### Off-Road Braking

Using the brakes to come to a complete standstill, or more typically to reduce your speed to a controllable level on a fast downhill stretch, is a tricky matter under off-road conditions. Firstly, the slope may be so steep that you tend to topple forward easily, while at the same time you have to deal with the inevitable ac-

celerating effect caused by the downslope. Secondly, the less predictable road surface may greatly reduce the traction between the tires and the ground. Finally, you may have to brake while at the same time avoiding an obstacle.

Before going downhill, get ready for it. Put your seat low down, which is easily done if you have a Hite-Rite seat post adjusting spring guide. Sit far back on the seat and hold back, keeping a low profile, the pedals horizontal. The single most frequently made mistake amongst novices is to let one or even both legs dangle, with the pedals either dangling freely or in top and bottom position.

Get a feel for how much braking force is enough. While going straight down, you can use both brakes, but on a very long slope you may want to use them intermittently, to keep both of them effective. As long as the road is not too steep, you can probably get by applying only one brake. That may be the front brake as long as you are going straight. When deviating one way or the other, try to brake just enough before you get to the curve, so you don't need to do so while leaning. If you do have to brake while leaning in a curve, only apply the one in the rear – gently.

Try to stay relaxed, rather than tensing up in a cramped position, so you follow the bike and its movements. That way you will soon learn to balance the amount of braking necessary with the accompanying weight shifts needed to keep control over the bike. Don't feel you have to be braking all the time: just keep down to a speed that is low enough to give you control in critical locations. That may mean braking rather vigorously on certain sections, where the surface is good and the route straight, letting the bike gather momentum again up to the next controllable stretch.

### Downhill Switchbacks

Often in off-road situations, you will have to somehow get down slopes that seem too steep and too rough to ride straight down. For the time being they probably are, but there are ways around this problem. Instead of roaring straight down the shortest way, you can use the same technique applied in downhill skiing where you shift your weight from side to side, following what is essentially a switchback course.

The same can be done on a bike. You ride along the contour of the grade, dropping elevation only slightly, deviating from your eventual destination. Then you shift your weight in a very sharp forced turn towards the opposite side. This way, you never reach the murderous speed induced by a straight downhill course. Instead, you stay within a reasonable speed. This maneuver is tricky, so you'd better practice it. As your confidence develops, you will be able to handle higher and higher speeds, requiring fewer and fewer turns to get down the hill.

Start this kind of practice on a relatively wide downhill stretch, where you have plenty of room to deviate one way or the other. Point your bike down only slightly under an angle, so you are riding along the side of the hill, rather than straight down. Sometime before your speed gets too high, but while still going straight, apply the front and rear brakes together briefly, immediately followed by the steering action and the necessary shift of weight to the downhill side, to induce a forced turn.

Repeat this maneuver in the opposite direction, again shifting your weight to the uphill side. This way, you make another sharp turn, back the same direction as at first. Continue criss-crossing down the hillside until you get down. It will take you a long

Trials expert David Arbogast showing how you make your bike fly at Howorth Park in Santa Rosa, California. (Photo Donald Favello)

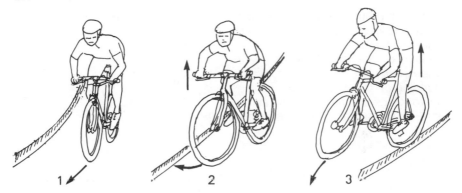

Fig. 8.2 Jumping sideways

time, compared to what it would have taken to roll straight down, and perhaps you picked a slope you could have handled that way. However, you'll have gained a lot of practice and once you can do it down a gentle slope, you will feel confident trying it down a steeper one. With a few days' deliberate practice, you can learn to do this so well that you can get down quite steep slopes.

### Off-Road Climbing
In Chapter 7 you have learned how to cycle uphill one of two ways: spinning fast in a relatively low gear for the slope, and standing on the pedals, 'honking' uphill in a relatively high gear for that slope. When cycling off-road, another factor has to be considered: in addition to otherwise unheard-of grades, you have to get used to riding in loose soil, rather than smooth asphalt or other surfaces that offer high and consistent traction.

Though your mountain bike probably has the kind of rubber on its wheels that provides as much traction as you can get, the conditions riding up steep slopes are a little tricky. This is due to the combined effect of loose or unpredictable surfaces and the extreme steepness of the grade. As you go uphill, your center of gravity shifts back on the bike. Though this improves traction by increasing the load on the rear wheel, it also reduces the load on the front wheel to such an extent that your steering becomes less predictable.

When you stand on the pedals on a steep uphill stretch, your weight is relatively far back, and that may unload the front wheel so much that the bike gets out of control, beginning to lift off or shift sideways. With the first trace of this, lean a little further forward, bending the arms a little to lean on the handlebars. Not too far, though, keeping enough weight on the rear wheel to ensure traction. It all becomes a subtle play, balancing your weight by minute forward and backward shifts to keep the front wheel on the ground, while retaining traction in the back.

### Jumping the Bike
Another weird but useful act for off-road cycling situations is making first the front, then the rear wheel jump over an obstacle. You may have to do this when there is an unavoidable obstacle ahead of you. It's a matter of shifting your weight back and forth to lift the appropriate wheel off the ground. To jump up, first throw your weight backwards, while pulling up on the handlebars to lift the front wheel. At the same time accelerate vigorously, by pushing hard on the forward,

pedal. With some practice, you'll soon be able to lift the front end of the bike at least a foot up in the air.

Next, do the same with the rear wheel, throwing your weight forward, standing on the pedals, while pulling up your legs and bottom at the same time. This is harder, but it can be mastered. Finally, practice coordinating the two shifts, so that you first lift the front and then, as soon as you've reached the highest point, start raising the back. After some time, you should be able to actually make the bike fly, lifting both wheels in such short sequence that the rear wheel comes off the ground well before the front wheel comes down.

One variant of this technique is the art of jumping up sideways, which may be needed to handle obstacles like ridges and tracks that run nearly parallel to the road. To do this, the bike has to be forced to move sideways in a short and snappy diversion just preceding the jump. Do that by combining the diversion technique described above under *Avoiding Obstacles* with the jump. Fig. 8.2 shows how this can be done.

Get close to the ridge you want to jump, riding parallel to it. Then briefly steer away from the ridge. This immediately causes the bike to lean towards the obstacle. Now catch yourself by steering sharply in that same direction, lifting the front wheel when you are close to the obstacle, immediately followed by the rear wheel. Practice is all it takes, and the empty parking lot with a chalk line as a substitute ridge will be the best place to

Fig. 8.3 Riding through a depression

do that, before you attempt it under real off-road conditions, at least if you are a little hesitant about it. Of course, many people prefer to get their first practice out amongst the trees and rocks. Wear a helmet and gloves, wherever you practice.

### Riding Through a Depression

Sometimes you will have to ride through a ditch, a big pothole or some other depression. To do that with minimal risk to bike and rider, you can use something akin to the jumping technique. Enter the depression with your weight near the front of the bike. Then lift the front wheel by throwing your weight back and pulling up the handlebars, just before the front wheel hits the lowest point of the depression. Finally, ride up the other side and pull up the rear, while shifting your weight to the front of the bike to climb back out. In open terrain, select your route through the depression so as to avoid too abrupt a drop and subsequent climb, as illustrated in Fig. 8.3.

# 9
# Bicycle Safety and Health

Bicycling – whether done on the road, on trails or cross-country – is not an entirely riskless undertaking. Neither are many other pursuits: accidents and other health hazards are very real risks everywhere. In this chapter you will be shown how to minimize the risks you are exposed to when riding your mountain bike.

In any discussion about bicycle safety, the main subject of interest seems to be the presumed danger of being involved in a collision with a motor vehicle. In off-road cycling that risk is rather remote, although it must be remembered that most mountain bikes are ridden on ordinary roads most of the time. However, even off-road, the risk is not reduced to zero: there are many hazards that have nothing to do with motor vehicles. Following the advice in this chapter, you can learn to avoid most of the dangers, minimizing injuries and staying healthy riding your bike.

Considering the various hazards, ranging from those to your own body and equipment to the harm or loss you may cause others, it may be smart to take out some kind of insurance. Personal liability insurance is perhaps the most important. In addition, you may want to make sure you have adequate health insurance to cover the danger of falls or collisions.

It would be a good idea to learn how to deal with accidents, injuries, sickness and other health related emergencies while cycling or touring. Do you really know what to do when you are bleeding, when you think you may have broken something, when one of your companions faints or is seriously hurt? Take a first aid course

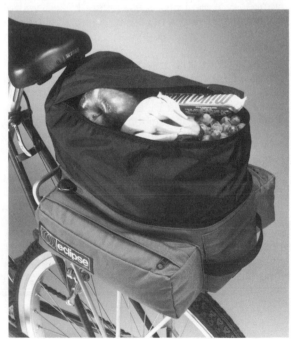

Rack-top bag by Eclipse. Bags like this, provided mounted firmly and well packed, are particularly suitable for off-road use, since they don't get in your way, as most pannier bags do.

to be prepared for dealing with the un-anticipated. That is a lot smarter than shutting your eyes, hoping nothing serious will happen. Even if you are spared yourself, you may be able to save someone else's life. If you can't take a first aid course, at least read up on the subject – appropriate literature is included in the Bibliography.

### The Risks of Bicycling

A lot of research has been done in recent years on the subject of bicycle accidents and injuries. Some of these studies dealt specifically with bicycle touring, such as the survey by Jerrold Kaplan on the injuries reported during the first year of the Bikecentennial program. Other reports are largely based on either day-to-day cycling experiences typical in an urban environment, or on the accidents reported by club cyclists, racers or students. To summarize the available evidence in a nutshell, the majority of bicycle accidents are attributable to a very limited number of typical mistakes, most of which can be avoided or counteracted by intelligent cycling techniques.

### Off-road Dangers

What may astonish most people at first is the implicit conclusion from several of these studies that the risk of being involved in an accident is greater on trails and paths than on roads with motor traffic. Keep this in mind when riding off-road. Many of the very characteristics that make cross-country cycling so enjoyable are also responsible for the increased risk.

Whereas roads are designed for wheeled vehicles travelling at speed, the back country is not – fortunately, in a way. Realize this when cycling, so you are prepared at all times to react to the unevenness of the surface, soft or slippery sections, ridges and various other obstacles. Anticipate emerging wildlife, hikers, rangers or bicyclists, who may suddenly appear from around the next bend or from behind a bush or rocky outcrop. Practice the control of your bike as outlined in the preceding chapters, so you can react to the unexpected and regain control over your bike even under difficult conditions. Braking, steering, yes even falling gracefully, can all be practiced and perfected.

### Protective Gear

The need for protective gear should be just as obvious in off-road cycling as it is while riding in traffic. Wear a helmet, gloves and perhaps long sleeved and long legged garments, preferably double layers. Helmets are not some magic cure against motorists running into you, as some cyclists seem to think. They serve to stop you from cracking your skull or damaging its contents when you fall off the bike – and you're likely to fall off your bike more than once when travelling in the outback.

If you fall on your head in any kind of fall or collision, the impact tends to smash the brain against the inside of the skull, followed by the reverse action as it rebounds. The human brain can usually withstand this kind of treatment without lasting damage if the resulting deceleration does not exceed about 300 G or 3000 m/sec$^2$. Look at it this way: the head probably falls to the ground from a height of 1.5 m (5 ft). This results in a speed of 5 m/sec$^2$ at the time of impact. To keep the deceleration down below 3000 m/sec$^2$, this speed must be reduced to zero in no less than 0.002 sec.

Neither your skull, nor the object with which you collide is likely to deform gradually enough to achieve that kind of deceleration. That's why energy absorbing helmets with thick crushable foam shells were developed. Neither flexible nor hard materials will do the trick by themselves. It's not a bad idea to have a hard outer shell cover to distribute the effect of the impact, and it is nice to get some comfort inside from a soft flexible liner, but the crushing of about ¾ inch of seemingly brittle foam is essential to absorb the shock. The minimum requirements for a safe helmet are those specified in the American standard ANSI Z-90.4.

### Risk Evaluation

Perhaps the most important lesson to learn from the investigations dealing with the safety of touring cyclists is the correlation between risk and trip length found. Put simply, the likelihood of getting hurt – be it as a result of a traffic accident or a fall – increases dramatically after a daily distance of 70 miles on the road, much less under off-road conditions. This applies especially to cyclists carrying luggage and handling difficult terrain, and most dramatically to inexperienced riders. Hence the following advice: if you are new to cycling, keep your daily distance down to no more than 70 road miles or 40 miles off-road to minimize the risk.

Another significant finding is that the more experienced cyclists have markedly fewer accidents, and can go longer distances. This is one good argument for gaining experience and skills as quickly as possible. Following the advice contained in the preceding chapters will not only increase the joy, satisfaction and effectiveness of cycling, it will also minimize the hazards.

### Falls and Collisions

In bicycle falls and collisions, virtually every injury to the cyclist results from the impact when the cyclist falls off the bike. He either hits the surface, an object on or along his path, another person or vehicle, or his own bike. Four

types of falls and collisions can be distinguished: stopping, diverting, skidding and loss of control. I shall describe these categories, followed by a few hints about preventing and treating the typical injuries that may result.

### Stopping Accidents

In a stopping accident, the bicycle runs into an obstacle that halts its progress. Depending on the cyclist's speed, the impact can be very serious. As the bicycle itself is stopped, inertia keeps the rider going forward, throwing him against or over the handlebars. The kinetic energy of the moving mass will be dissipated very suddenly, often in an unfortunate location. Your genitals may hit the handlebar stem or your skull may hit the ground or the object with which the bike collided.

The way to guard yourself against these accidents is to look and think

Wear a helmet, if you value the contents of your skull – even the author does.

ahead, so you don't run into any obstacles. If necessary, control your speed to allow handling the unexpected when a potential danger may be looming up around the next corner. Learn to apply the diverting technique described in the preceding chapter. The way to minimize the impact of the most serious form of stopping accident is to wear an energy absorbing helmet.

## Diverting Accidents

A diverting accident occurs when the front wheel is pushed sideways by an external force, while the rider is not leaning in the same direction to regain balance. Typical causes off-road are rocky ridges, while on roads the same effects are caused by railway tracks, cracks in the road surface, the edge of the road, and by touching another rider's rear wheel with your front wheel. The result is that you fall sideways and hit the ground or some obstacle by the side of your path. Depending how unexpectedly it happens, you may be able to break the fall by stretching out an arm, which seems to be an automatic reflex in this situation.

Characteristic injuries range from abrasions and lacerations of the hands and the sides of arms and legs to bruised hips and sprained or broken wrists. More serious cases, usually incurred at higher speeds, may involve broken collarbones and injuries to the face or the side of the skull. The impact of lesser injuries can be minimized by wearing padded gloves and double layers of clothing with long sleeves and pants. Wearing a helmet will minimize damage to the side of the head.

Diverting accidents can often be avoided if the cyclist is both careful and alert. Keep an eye out for the typical danger situations. Don't overlap wheels with other riders, don't approach surface ridges under a shallow angle. A last second diversion can often be made along the lines of the diverting technique described in Chapter 8. In the case of a ridge in the surface, use the technique of sideways jumping, also described there. When your front wheel touches the rear wheel of another rider, or if your handlebars are pushed over by an outside force, you may sometimes save the day if you react by immediately leaning in the direction you were diverted, and then steer to regain control.

## Skidding Accidents

When the bicycle keeps going, or moves off in an unintended direction, despite your efforts to brake or steer, it will be due to skidding between the tires and the road surface. This happens more frequently when the surface is loose or wet, but may also be caused by moisture, frost, loose sand or fallen leaves. Under these conditions, sudden diversions or movements, hard braking and excessive lean when cornering may all cause skidding either forward or sideways.

Skidding accidents often cause the cyclist to fall sideways, resulting in abrasions, lacerations or, more rarely, fractures. Avoid skidding by checking the road surface ahead and avoiding sudden steering or braking maneuvers and excessive leaning in curves. Cross slick patches, ranging from loose gravel and wet rocks off-road to railway tracks, sand, leaves or even white road markings on regular roads, with the bicycle upright. Carry out the requisite steering and balancing actions before you reach such danger spots.

If you can not avoid it, once you feel you are entering a skid, try to move your weight towards the back of the bike as much as possible, sliding back on the saddle and stretching the arms. Follow the bike, rather than trying to force it back. Finally, don't do what seems an obvious reaction to the less experienced, namely getting off the saddle to straddle the top tube with one leg dangling. As with so many cycling techniques, skidding can be practiced in a relatively safe environment such as an empty parking lot.

### Loss of Control Accidents

At higher speeds, especially in a steep descent, loss of control accidents sometimes occur. In this case, you can't steer the bike the way you intend to go. This happens when you find yourself having to steer in one direction when you are leaning the other way, or when speed control braking initiates unexpected oscillations. This situation often develops into a fall or collision along the lines of one of the two accident types described above.

Prevention is only possible with experience: don't go faster than the speed at which you feel in control. The more you ride under various situations, the more you will develop a feel for what is a safe speed, when to brake and how to steer to maintain control over the bike. Once the situation sets in, try to keep your cool. Don't panic. Follow the bike, rather than forcing it over. The worst thing you can do is to tense up and get off the saddle. Stay in touch with handlebars, seat and pedals, steering in the direction of your lean. This way, you may get out of it without falling or colliding, though your nerves may have suffered.

### Traffic Hazards

In this section we shall discuss in detail what most upset at least one reviewer about the first edition of this book: the fact that I treat bicycle traffic safety in a mountain bike book. Paradoxical though it may seem at first, I feel it is justified, since most mountain bikes are ridden as much in traffic as they are off-road. Besides, it's the danger of cycling in traffic that scares off most beginners from the sport. Cycling on regular roads does not have to be as dangerous as it seems. You can learn to handle it, since traffic is nothing but people moving. Since you are human yourself and smart enough to understand the laws of physics, you can learn to avoid the risks associated with such an environment – on your bike as much as in your car.

In the Bikecentennial survey of long distance touring cyclists, two fatal accidents occurred. However, fatal accidents are only a small percentage of all injuries, and numerous other serious accidents do occur. Though the majority of all injured cyclists are themselves to blame for their injuries, there will always be some accidents that are directly attributable to bullying and inconsiderate motorists.

She is just posing for the picture: riding on the wrong side is one way to get into trouble, even on a quiet road.

Unfortunately, this type of accident forms a high proportion of those that experienced cyclists encounter. These riders have learned to handle their machines rationally and safely in traffic, virtually eliminating their risk concerning the more common kind of accidents to which the incompetent are exposed. But they are just as vulnerable to the remaining irrational dangers of the road.

The only defense against inconsiderate road users is not to provoke them. Give in, even if it seems highly unfair. It's an unequal battle and sometimes it's smarter not to insist on justice. You will encounter fewer of these particular risks if you avoid the situations where they are most likely: Sunday afternoons and late evenings, when many boisterous drunks are on the road. Oddly enough, these accidents are also more likely on lightly travelled roads near small towns than in heavy traffic near a big city. Though I realize that the latter condition does not make the ideal bicycle touring environment, try to avoid the quiet roads near small towns at high-risk times.

Most accidents, of course, are not of this type. They simply happen when two people each make a mistake: one initiates a wrong move, and the other fails to react in such a way that a collision is avoided. Keep that in mind when cycling. Remain alert for possible mistakes others may make, and try to avoid taking unexpected or inconsiderate actions yourself as much as humanly possible. Anticipate not only the predictable, but also the unexpected: the motorist looming behind the next corner or intersection, the dog appearing from a driveway, or the bicyclist suddenly crossing your path in the dark without lights.

The latter subject deserves special attention. The only way to arm yourself is to make sure you do not cycle out after dark without lights, so at least you can be seen. Proper lighting on the bike is needed in addition to the curiously ineffective array of reflectors that is increasingly prescribed by law in various countries. The gravest danger of reflectors lies in the inappropriate impression they give of making you highly visible. In reality, several of them only make you visible to those who do not endanger you anyway. A bright light in the front and a big rear light or reflector facing back are essential, while all the other goodies won't do a thing that the former wouldn't do more effectively.

Most accidents occur in daylight, even though the relative risk is greater at night. Whether by day or night, cycle with all your senses alert. In general, ride your bike as you would drive your car, always verifying whether the road ahead of you is clear, and taking particular care to select your path wisely at junctions and intersections. As a relatively slow vehicle, you must look behind you, to ascertain that nobody is following closely, before you move over into another traffic lane or away from your previous path.

Forget anything you ever heard about bikes being different from motor vehicles. As a wheeled vehicle, your bike answers to the same laws of physics as does your car. Adhere to the most basic rules of traffic you learned to handle a car, and you'll be safe on a bike. No doubt the worst advice ever given to cyclists in many parts of the US is to ride on the side of the road where a pedestrian would walk, namely facing traffic. On a bike, you *are* the traffic, and you belong on the same side as all other vehicles travelling the same way.

The rules of the road as applied to motor vehicles are based on a system that has evolved gradually and logically. This system works the way it does because it is logical. If it is

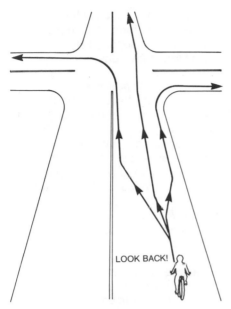

LOOK BACK!

Fig. 9.1 Turning in traffic

dangerous for motorists to do certain things, then it will be at least as dangerous on a bike. This applies equally when travelling abroad, although it will be smart to prepare for the peculiar kind of laws that have been instituted in some societies which relegate bicyclists to an inferior (and invariably more dangerous) place on the road.

Don't hug the curb but claim your place on the road. Your place is somewhere to the right of the centerline of the path normally taken by cars on a wide road (assuming RH traffic). Keep at least 90 cm (3 ft) away from the inside edge, even if the road is too narrow to stay clear to the right of the normal path of motor vehicles. Don't dart in and out around parked vehicles and other obstructions along the side of the road. When making a turn, adhere to the method outlined in Fig. 9.1. Thus, to go straight at an intersection, make sure you will not be overtaken by vehicles turning right. To turn right, get close to the RH edge. To

turn left, choose a path near the center of the road or the middle of a traffic lane marked for that direction well before the actual intersection, after having established that you will not be cutting across the path of vehicles following closely behind.

Excessive attention is often paid to hand signals in traffic education for cyclists. Yes, when cycling on the road, you should signal your intention before you do things like diverting, turning off or slowing down. That applies particularly when cycling with others in a group, where the first person should also point out and audibly identify obstacles or hazards in the road. But avoid the dangerous habit of assuming a hand signal will ward off danger. Your hand is not a magic wand, and if somebody is following so closely that you can signal to him your intention of turning across his path, you should not do it. Instead, wait until your maneuver does not interfere with traffic following closely behind.

The most feared type of bicycle accident is the one that involves being hit from behind. These accidents do happen, and both the fatal accidents that occurred during the Bikecentennial survey were of this type. Though there is hardly any possible defense to ward them off, it is worth considering that they are characterized by a number of common factors. They invariably occur on otherwise deserted roads, where the attention of motorist and cyclist alike are at a low, since both feel perfectly secure.

Inconspicuous clothing, a low sun, blinding one or both participants, and a lack of the cyclist's awareness, due to tiredness at the end of a long day, are also common features. It may be smart to increase your conspicuity. Wearing bright colors, such as yellow, pink, orange or bright green, may well help others spot you in time to avoid this type of accident.

## Treating Injuries

In this and the following sections, you will be shown how to treat or limit the effect of several typical bicycle injuries. The most common type of injuries are abrasions, referred to in cycling club circles as road rash, even when incurred off-road. They usually heal relatively fast, though they can be quite painful. Wash out the wound with water and soap, and remove any particles of road dirt to prevent infection. There may be a risk of tetanus if the wound draws blood. Even if you have been immunized against tetanus before, get a tetanus shot within 24 hours if the last one was over two years ago.

If you have never been immunized before, get a full immunization, consisting of two (different) shots within 24 hours, followed by two more after two weeks and six months, respectively. Apply a dressing only if the location is covered by clothing, since the wound will heal faster when exposed to air. Avoid the formation of a scab by treating the wound with an antibiotic salve. See a doctor if any signs of infection occur, such as swelling, itching or fever.

## Sprained Limbs

In case of a fall, your tendency to stick out an arm to break the impact may result in a sprained or even a fractured wrist. In other accident situations this can also happen to the knee or the ankle. Spraining is really nothing but damage to the ligaments that surround and hold the various parts of a joint together. Typical symptoms are a local sensation of heat, itching and swelling.

Whenever possible, keep the area cold with an ice bag. Get professional medical advice if you feel a stinging pain or if fever develops, because it may actually be a fracture that was at first incorrectly diagnosed as a sprain.

This may be the case when the fracture takes the form of a simple 'clean' crack without superficially visible deformation of the bone.

## Fractures

Typical cycling fractures are those of the wrist and the collarbone, both caused when falling: the one when extending the arm to break the fall, the other when you don't have time to do that. You or medical personnel may not at first notice a clean fracture as described above: there may not be any outward sign.

If there is a stinging pain when the part is moved or touched, I suggest you get an X-ray to make sure, even if a fracture is not immediately obvious. You'll need medical help to set and bandage the fracture, and you must give up cycling until it is healed, which will take about five weeks. Sad if that happens during a bicycle tour, but better than continuing in agony.

## Other Health Problems

The remaining part of this chapter will be devoted to the health hazards of cycling that have nothing to do with falling off the bike. We will look at the most common complaints and discuss some methods of prevention, as well as possible cures. This brief description can not cover the entire field. Nor should most of the issues discussed here be generalized too lightly. The same symptoms may have different causes in different cases; conversely, the same cure may not work for two superficially similar problems. Yet in most cases the following remarks will apply.

## Saddle Sores

Though beginning bicyclists may at first feel uncomfortable on the bike seat, they have no idea what kind of agony real seat problems can bring. As soon as any pressure is applied, when you sit on a bike seat, things will get worse. Avoid the most serious seat problems by taking it easy for one or two days when symptoms start to develop. During the hours you spend in the saddle, the combined effect of perspiration, pressure and chafing may cause cracks in the skin, where bacteria can enter. The result can be anything from a mild inflammation to the most painful boils.

There is of course little chance of healing as long as you continue riding vigorously. Prevention and early relief are the methods to combat saddle sores. The clue to both is hygiene. Wash and dry both your crotch and your cycling shorts after every day's ride. Many bicyclists also treat the affected areas with rubbing alcohol, which both disinfects and increases the skin's resistance to chafing, or with talcum powder, which prevents further damage.

You'll need at least two pairs of cycling shorts on a longer tour or when going on frequent day rides, so you can always rely on a clean, dry pair when you start out. Wash them out, taking particular care to get the chamois clean, and hang them out to dry thoroughly, preferably outside, where the sun's ultraviolet rays act to kill any remaining bacteria. Treat the chamois with either talcum powder or a special treatment for that purpose. I prefer to use a water soluble cream, such as Noxema, since it is easier to wash out.

The quality of your saddle and your riding position also affect the development of crotch problems. If early symptoms appear in the form of redness or soreness, consider getting a softer saddle, sitting further to the back of your saddle, or lowering the handlebars a little to reduce the pressure on the seat. If the problem gets out of hand, take a rest from cycling until the sores have fully healed.

## Knee Problems

Because the cycling movement does not apply the high impacting shock load on the legs that is associated with running, it's surprising that knee problems are so prevalent. They are concentrated mainly with two groups of cyclists: beginners and very strong, muscular riders. In both cases, the cause seems to be pushing too high a gear. This strains the knee joint, resulting in damage to the membranes that separate the moving portions of the joint and the ligaments holding the bits and pieces of the joint together. In cold weather the problems get aggravated, so it would be wise to wear long pants whenever the temperature is below 18°C (65°F), especially if fast descents are involved.

Butt saver: a really comfortable saddle like the Brooks 66 Champion can prevent serious seat problems.

Prevent excessive forces on the knee joint by gearing so low that you can spin lightly under all conditions. Avoid climbing in the saddle with pedalling speeds below 60 RPM. Equip your bicycle with the kind of gear ratios that allow you to do that, and choose a lower gear whenever necessary. Once the problem has developed, either giving up cycling or riding loosely in low gears will aid the healing process. I suggest you continue cycling in very low gears, spinning freely. That will probably prepare you to get back into shape, while forcing you to avoid the high gears that caused the problem in the first place.

### Tendonitus

This is an infection of the Achilles tendon, which attaches the big muscle of the lower leg, the gastrocnemius, to the heel bone. It is an important tendon in cycling, since it transmits the

One of the most unusual mountain bikes is this Slingshot machine. Despite its built in spring, it has astonishing directional stability.

pedalling force to the foot. It sometimes gets damaged or torn under the same kind of circumstances as described above for knee injuries: cycling with too much force in too high a gear. The problem is aggravated by low temperatures, which explains why it generally develops in the early season.

To avoid tendonitus, wear long woollen socks whenever the temperature is below 18°C (65°F). It may also help to wear shoes that come up quite high, maximizing the support they provide. Get used to riding with a supple movement in a low gear, which is the clue to preventing many cycling complaints. Healing requires rest, followed by a return to cycling with minimum pedal force in a low gear.

### Numbness

Beginning cyclists, not used to riding long distances, sometimes develop a loss of feeling in certain areas of contact with the bike. The most typical location is the hands, but it also occurs in the feet and the crotch. The numb feeling is caused by excessive and

unvaried prolonged pressure on the nerves and blood vessels. The effects are usually relieved with rest, though they have at times been felt for several days.

Once the problem develops, get relief by changing your position frequently, moving the hands from one part of the handlebars to another, or moving from one area of the seat to the other if the crotch is affected. To prevent numbness in the various locations, use well padded gloves, foam hand grips, a soft saddle in a slightly higher position, or thick soled shoes with cushioned inner soles, laced loosely at the bottom but tightly higher up, so the foot does not slip forward to push the toe against the front of the shoe.

### Back Ache
Many riders complain of aches in the back, the lower neck and the shoulders, especially early in the season. These are probably attributable to insufficient training of the muscles. It is largely the result of unfamiliar isometric muscle work, keeping still in a forward bent position. This condition is also aggravated by low temperatures, so it is wise to wear warm bicycle clothing in cool weather.

To avoid the early-season reconditioning complaints, the best remedy is not to stop cycling in winter. Two rides a week at a moderate pace, or extended use of a home trainer with a proper low riding position, will do the trick. Alternately, you may start off in the new season with a slightly higher handlebar position and once more a low gear. Sleeping on a firm mattress and keeping warm also seems to help either alleviate or prevent the problem.

### Sinus and Bronchial Complaints
In the cooler periods, many cyclists develop breathing problems, originating either in the sinuses or the bronchi. The same may happen when a rider used to cycling at sea level gets into the mountains, where the cold air in a fast descent can be very unsettling. It's generally attributable to undercooling, the only solution being to dress warmer and to cycle slowly enough to allow breathing through the nose.

After a demanding climb in cooler weather, do not strip off warm clothing, open your shirt or drink excessive quantities of cold liquids, even if you sweat profusely. All these things may cause more rapid cooling than your

Ultraspec: stylish and functional eye protection from Rhode Gear. These items keep sun, wind, dust and insects out of your eyes. Several models fit over the top of prescription glasses.

body can handle. You will cool off gradually and without impairing your health, if you merely reduce your output and allow the sweat to evaporate naturally through the fibers of your bicycle clothing. This works best if you wear clothing that contains a high percentage of wool.

## Sun Burn

When bicycling on a clear day, you will be exposed to the sun for many hours at a stretch. Unless you have a naturally high resistance to ultra violet rays, exposed parts of the body are likely to suffer sun burn. To prevent it, use a sun tan lotion with a protection factor of 15. This means that only one fifteenth of the ultra violet rays reach the skin. Even more effective is a zinc oxide based protection, applied on particularly exposed locations such as the nose, the ears and the neck.

Sun burn is just that: a burn, and that means it should be treated like any other burn. Cold water, and perhaps a light dressing such as baby oil, is all you can do, apart from waiting for it to heal. There are substances that suppress the pain, but that is all they do: they don't heal the injury. In really severe cases, sun burn can be serious enough to justify professional medical care.

# Where to Ride Your Mountain Bike

It may seem curious to devote a chapter to a question that perhaps shouldn't be asked: the mountain bike is supposed to go anywhere. Still, you may benefit from a little advice about riding in the kind of terrain where it can display its strengths most impressively.

It does to some extent depend on what kind of mountain bike you have selected – a trail bike, a downhill rocket, a street cruiser, what have you. Mountain bike or not, any bicycle is most efficient, and therefore most enjoyable ridden, on hard, dry, smooth and level ground. That may contradict what you've heard about the mountain bike before, but it's useful to keep in mind.

### Getting Out There
Don't feel that a mountain bike must be transported to the trailhead in the back of a pick-up or on the roof of your car, to be unloaded and returned after use. Any bike, including your fat-tired machine, is a means of transportation. It is intended to get you from A to B. The mountain bike can do this on roads as well as off-road, but there's no need to shun using the machine to get from your house to some point in the woods, nor to use it for shopping, commuting and any of the other potential uses for which I have been using my various bikes as long as I can remember.

What's nice about riding off-road is not a function of the roughness, the dirt or any of the other characteristics of the terrain. Instead, you relish the remoteness, the solitude, the experience of nature and the lack of traffic. Without these, even a mountain bike is not more enjoyable on rough roads than on smooth ones. So, unless you

Though this picture and a lot of other publicity may lead you to believe differently, you can *ride* your mountain bike to the trail head. I for one think that bikes should be ridden rather than trucked.

go for the challenge, select the most direct, smoothest, hardest, driest and most level surface that can be used to get you from A to B.

Keeping that in mind, we can now concentrate on the kind of terrain for which your mountain bike is more suitable than any other machine known to man. The argument that you may put in 80 percent of your mileage or more on paved roads should not necessarily discourage you from getting the kind of equipment that is best suited to rough riding. After all, that enjoyable remaining 20% is probably why you got this particular kind of bike. The thickest tires and the strongest forks don't detract from your riding pleasure on paved roads as much as they benefit you off-road.

### Characteristics for Use
Let's look a little closer at some characteristics of the mountain bike and deduce how it can best be utilized. Subsequently, we'll dig into the off-road riding environment a little more deeply. On smooth roads your mountain bike is only marginally less efficient than a skinny tired ten-speed, especially at moderate riding speeds.

In traffic, especially in an urban environment, it has some significant advantages: the brakes are easy within your reach and the more upright position gives you a better overview of the road ahead. On the other hand, the slightly higher weight makes it a little more sluggish and more tiring to accelerate frequently, as needed in stop-and-go traffic.

The fat tires mean you have to worry less about where you ride and what you traverse. Cracks, potholes and other obstacles in the road that would throw you off the skinny tired machine will hardly leave their mark when riding the mountain bike. Assuming the right racks and packs, carrying luggage is a cinch, due to the sturdy construction and the generous geometry.

The slight disadvantages relative to the ten-speed at higher riding speeds are more hypothetical than real to most riders. In a recent survey I conducted of riding posture, it was found that over 75% of ten-speed riders selected such a poor posture that they did not benefit one bit from their equipment. You can do as well or better on a mountain bike and have its advantages to boot.

If you really want the benefit of the lower riding position that comes from drop bars, there is nothing to stop you from modifying your mountain bike by installing the appropriate handlebars. As for the fat tires, as long as you ride on the road, you can inflate them as hard as the skinny tires of most ten-speeds. Believe it or not, rolling resistance is not directly related to tire width, but solely to pressure: the harder the tire, the easier the ride.

Exploit the advantages and other characteristics of your mountain bike wherever you can, so you get the full benefit and maximum enjoyment out of your equipment. If I were to select just one bike for all uses, I would probably select a mountain bike. That's because it is the most universal machine. It does anything my other bikes can do, most things almost as well, some better, and some that the other bikes can't do at all. What other bikes can't do as well as the mountain bike will be the subject of the remainder of this chapter.

### Uphill-Downhill Riding
In most parts of the US and Canada, and perhaps even more so in the rest of the world, there is suitable terrain for real off-road riding within easy cycling reach, wherever you live. So you can ride there and back. This will give you considerably more cycling experience than you would otherwise

get. Besides, it's a lot simpler than dealing with loading and unloading bikes and returning to the place where you parked your car.

Open hillsides or those with rough trails dropping down steeply can be found in many areas. The mountain bike's characteristics definitely lend it superbly to this kind of use. In fact, that's how the mountain bike was born. The first mountain bike riders did little more (or less) with their machines than ride them down steep, unpaved hillsides at a murderous pace, only to struggle their way up again to start all over.

This kind of uphill-downhill riding is most enjoyable as a group activity. Having tried it by myself, I must admit it is about as boring as it sounds, whereas the company, the mutual encouragement, the fun of it all, makes it more exciting when in the company of others. In addition, it is more educational: you may never learn the proper control over your bike and its movements, unless you can gauge your own progress with that of others.

Consider the environmental impact and the legality of what you are doing, though. If there is an ordinance against it, chances are it's not merely to spoil your fun, but rather to prevent you from doing damage to the natural environment. What some of this riding does to the watershed characteristics of the terrain can be quite serious. Though I don't believe mountain biking is the direct cause of the California mud slides of recent years, it may well have been a contributing factor in some cases.

If you are new to the sport, the best places to do downhill riding are probably known to others who ride mountain bikes. If nobody can put you on the right track for uphill-downhill riding, find your own site. You'll be surprised in what unlikely places you can find quite acceptable slopes. I even

found several places within cycling range from my parents' home in Holland, which is a proverbially flat country. It needn't be a thousand-foot drop: riding down the embankment of a high bridge ramp or a pile of soil next to a building site may do the trick for fun and practice.

Although you won't find another 'Repack', that famous Northern California slope that drops 1300 feet in less than two miles, you might discover quite a respectable little slope. After all, some of the most challenging and enjoyable slopes in off-road cycling are only one or two hundred feet high. You're not looking for the ultimate challenge all the time, you're just out to do your thing.

Looks more rustic than it is: the author's son climbing a man made hill right at the edge of town.

## Trail Riding

A lot of mountain bike riding has nothing to do with racing down steep hills. For those who are more into peace and solitude, cycling on unpaved roads and trails is the more mind-expanding experience. It's my kind of riding, largely because I'm a cautious old cat, who has taken all the unnecessary risks in his day and wants to live to tell others about it. Not only because I'm a coward: there is a distinct thrill to relaxed riding where there is no bustle and roar of cars to interrupt the tranquility, where all the obstacles are of God's creation, rather than man's.

Although I prefer to cycle alone or with one companion, this activity is not the exclusive domain of recluses and hermits. In fact, some of the major organized off-road events, with hundreds of participants, are of this kind. To find the right terrain for non-organized trail biking, there isn't a better tool than the topographical map, referred to as Geological Survey map in the US, Ordnance Survey in Britain.

This kind of map shows all trails, paths and roads, while the road map will show you which of these are paved and used for motor traffic. The difference is your exclusive domain, apart from any right-of-way restrictions you may have to contend with. In fact, access and right-of-way are the two intangibles in trail cycling these days. The sport is getting too popular too fast, and in defense or out of fear, authorities have banned cyclists from many potentially suitable areas.

You will probably use forest service or fire roads and trails intended for hikers most of the time. Don't stray off these trails, since this may cause damage, both to the environment and to our reputation. As long as you stay on the trails and do it with a modicum of consideration for others, you have nothing to fear and should not risk being banned from them by public agencies.

## Securing Access

In the first edition of this book, I had included a couple of envious remarks about the relative success at gaining access as compared to equestrians, claiming the latter do more harm than we do. This provoked some harsh responses from fellow cyclists who are also equestrians. I stand corrected: cyclists and equestrians have some of the same problems, and fear or misunderstanding is the driving force behind the restriction of either sport.

Those on foot have a justified claim to the most comprehensive access, and cyclists would do well to do all they can to defer to them. I have witnessed both ridiculous pedestrian fear of anything on wheels or hooves, and totally brutal disregard of the right of those on foot. Be considerate, and team up with other responsible cyclists and equestrians to sway both the public and the authorities against instituting or enforcing unwarranted restrictive access rules.

Government authorities and public representatives at all levels are supposed to be accountable to all the people, including you and your mountain biking friends. If you have the right arguments and present them reasonably, chances are pretty good you'll be able to secure or retain access in most cases where you and your bike don't represent a serious threat to the environment.

Join forces with other potential users of the same terrain, such as hikers and equestrians. Try to emphasize that mountain bike riders are normal, responsible, mature adults who eat lots of apple pie and watch fireworks, rather than some weird bunch of near outlaws, who probably don't remember the words to the national anthem. It also helps to be a member of some recognized, dignified outdoor or conservation organization, and point this out whenever you present your case in public.

A particularly touchy issue is that of National Wilderness Areas and the even more obscure so-called National Wilderness Study Areas in the US. The latter are regions that are under consideration for future designation as Wilderness Areas. This makes them off-limits at a slight of hand, without the Government's obligation to do anything to protect or develop the area. Although the sign at the trailhead may only explicitly prohibit 'motor vehicles', you may soon run into some ranger who'll lay down the law.

That's because the 1964 Wilderness Act prohibits the use of 'motor vehicles and other forms of mechanical transport', while specifically permitting horseback riding. You or I may not think of the mountain bike as providing 'mechanical transportation', but Smokey probably does. It's a stupid regulation, clothed in very imprecise wording, so help get it changed: ask your favorite Member of Congress to raise the issue and do something about it.

## Fringe Areas

Not everybody has a National Wildlife Area, State Forest or National Forest on his doorstep, and in other countries these terms might as well be the names of holy places in Sanskrit. Lacking such facilities, as well as the peculiar problems associated with securing access to them, you may be satisfied to remember that you can ride on any kind of open terrain and unpaved road, without worrying about such controversial terrain.

On the fringes of just about every city and suburb, there are areas where paved roads are anything from sparse to non-existant. Such areas may not always be the most idyllic, but they are usually quite suitable for your kind of use. If they don't give you the solitude of nature, instead constantly reminding you of man's encroaching action upon God's work, at least they offer a superb training ground for more romantic rides when you do get the chance to ride out in the woods.

Their advantage is that such areas are invariably easily accessible, both in terms of distance and in the way the paved roads allow you to get out there in little time. Use the maps proposed in this chapter, and make the most of

Doubling up off-road. This fine Mountain Goat mountain bike tandem by Jeff Lindsay is an excellent choice for cycling two up on paved roads as well. Mountain bike wheels and oversize tubing make for strong and rigid tandems, wherever you ride.

the information that can be summized from them. Consult Chapter 12 for an explanation of the most effective ways of using the maps.

The ultimate way to find good off-road cycling terrain goes well beyond the use of the map. It's out there, riding your bike, that you will find the best places to do it. Don't be bashful about going beyond where you know the way or are sure you can find your way back. Personally, I am punished with a particularly poor sense of orientation. That has the advantage that I often stumble into – to me – totally new areas. Despite my handicap, I have always managed to return home alive, even satisfied, often finding really nice and different routes there and back. You should be able to do it too.

With your mountain bike, you can take on the hills, going up and going down, or you can go around them. You can go where other road users would not care to travel. These are the advantages of your particular mode of transport. Exploit them. Making the most of these advantages, fearing neither sweat nor agony, the true mountain bike rider quickly discovers enjoyable, scenic, sometimes even spectacular, routes away from regular roads. Get out there and enjoy it to the full.

# Off-Road Cycling as a Sport

The modern mountain bike is not only a practical means of transportation, but also a fascinating piece of sporting equipment. Its origin can be traced back directly to the casually competitive sport of downhill racing. Even today, with the number of mountain bikes sold each year surpassing the sales of all other adult bicycles combined, sporting competition still plays an important role, both in its technical development and in its actual use.

Traditional road and track racing remains firmly established internationally. But within the English speaking world mountain bike racing has found a distinct niche. It is both a popular participation sport and one in which accomplished riders are making money at least semi-professionally.

They're off! Though not officially billed as a mountain bike race, the competitive spirit seems to prevail at the Sonoma County Rockhopper held annually near Santa Rosa. (James Cassimus/Bicycle Sport photograph)

Perhaps the most fascinating aspect of mountain bike racing as a sport is the remarkably high rate of participation. Not only is the number of participants relative to spectators very high compared to other sports, there is another significant index that shows mountain bike riding to be a major sport. Compare, if you will, the number of ten-speed riders or joggers to those who participate in the corresponding disciplines competitively: not too many. In mountain bike riding, on the other hand, a strikingly high percentage of riders are also racers.

### Off-Road versus Cyclo-Cross

Bicycle racing through rough terrain has been a popular sport for many years, especially in Europe. Cyclo-cross bike racing, though also practiced in the US, has little in common with mountain biking. The latter has developed with little regard for this pursuit. They are two distinct sports.

In cyclo-cross, endearingly referred to as 'mud-plugging' in Britain, light and rather fragile drop handlebar rac-

ing bicycles are used. These are equipped to make them suitable for the job at hand. Like the mountain bike, they have derailleur gearing and usually cantilever brakes. But that's where the similarity ends: they are much lighter and more fragile, running on skinny tires.

The way these featherweights stand up to the abuse of off-road cycling is by means of timely replacement. In fact, this equipment replacement procedure is now driven to the point of absurdity. In many races, competitors not only change bikes after every lap of the short course, to give the mechanics a chance to get them back in working order, they may even show up with different bikes for different sections of the course. As is so often the case, American racers outdo their European mentors in this respect, turning the race into a mechanic's nightmare, scurrying bikes back and forth between fixing and wrecking them.

The modern mountain bike sport is in some way a healthy reaction to this obsession with equipment replacement. It makes it possible to complete a race with just one bike, a true test of both man and machine. The same bike that is used uphill will also go down, ride in sand and on rocks. Instead of being carried over lengthy sections of the course, as is customary in cyclo-cross, it will carry the rider most of the way.

It was probably the well-known California bike racer and mountain bike pioneer Gary Fisher, who first served notice that the mountain bike was for real – at a cyclo-cross race of all places. At the 1980 California Cyclo-Cross Championships, he showed up with his fat tire bike, and ran away with the senior championship title.

Though fat-tire bikes had done well in some cyclo-cross races before, this was the first big success for the concept of fat tires. It proved that the mountain bike can not only do things no other bike can do, it can also do things for which more specialized equipment is intended.

Though in recent years there has been a trend to narrower tires on mountain bikes, most off-road racing is still best handled on bikes with really wide tires. In Chapter 20 you will find some additional hints on the selection of tires for particular terrain, both in racing situations and elsewhere. In general, the softer the ground, the wider and softer the tires, and the rougher the ground the wider and harder the tires should be. Only when racing on hard and relatively smooth ground, are the narrower tires appropriate.

**Bike Racing Organizations**
In the US, the national racing organization, the USCF (United States Cycling Federation), has not been very quick to recognize the potential of mountain bike racing, repeating the same error made with respect to BMX some years earlier. Almost since its inception, mountain bike racing has largely been sponsored by NORBA, the National Off-Road Bicycle Association. Started in 1983 as a membership organization, the elected directors saw fit to actually sell the organization to one of its founding members – and with it the rights of its membership.

Though the new owner was a benevolent and honorable man, the principle of private ownership, unbeknown to most of the members, set an ugly precedent. The various conflicts with the USCF might have been resolved more elegantly and permanently if there had been at least a pretense of membership control. Glenn Odell, the first owner put a lot of time and effort into lobbying for access and gaining insurance for the membership, while his industry-backed entourage was more interested in competition and commerce.

The combined efforts of organizing races, controlling the membership, dealing with a board of advisers and fighting political battles were more than any man could carry out alone. Three years later the organization was sold to another individual and nasty squables soon started – in fact have not been resolved to date. It is my private hope that enough of the membership will get interested in the affairs of running their own organization to either take over or to form a really democratic, membership-run, off-road cycling organization.

## Off-Road Events

No, I can't teach you here how to race or how to be successful in any of the various off-road events becoming increasingly popular in the US and abroad. You learn by doing, and you improve by practice and training. To train effectively and to understand the development of the various skills involved, you are referred to my *Bicycle Racing Guide*. In this section, we'll merely compare the various forms of off-road competition.

All competitive off-road events offer the novice the unique opportunity of participating on equal terms with the best. Even though some form of differentiation, similar to the categorization that is established in USCF-sponsored racing, is creeping into the sport, most races are still open to all comers with the appropriate credentials, which may be no more than a liability waiver and a ten dollar bill.

Real national celebrities in the world of off-road racing may be within touching distance, at least at the beginning of a race: they move ahead fast, while the novices are fidgeting to get into the right gear. Since most of these events are not based on the principle of numerous laps around a compact course, typical for cyclo-cross racing, the slow riders don't get

Mountain bike pioneer Gary Fisher going full blast down Repack in the annual Repack Downhill Race. (Photo Donald Favello)

Off-road racer Jacquie Phelan, alias Alice B. Toeclips, one of America's fastest and toughest woman riders. Here she shows off her Cunningham aluminum framed bike, which weighs about half as much as you'd think looking at it.

in the way of faster ones. Though quite a few organizers are beginning to distinguish between the real gonzos and those of us who are out for the fun of it, this is not an athletic class society. Consequently, it is possible for a talented and determined newcomer to rise to stardom within a much shorter time than is customary or possible in regular bike racing.

### Downhill Racing

No doubt the oldest form of the mountain bike race, this is nothing but what the name implies: a scramble down a steep open hillside or trail. The terrain may be marked to show where you are supposed to ride and where you're not. Generally, all competitors start together on an open section of road some distance from the actual hill, in order to weed them out a little before the real work starts. Then you show how fast you can get down.

The larger the group, the more you have to rely, not only on pure riding skills, but also on conflict avoidance technique and luck. Sometimes this kind of race is not a mass start event but rather a time trial, where riders start at intervals, and each rider is timed individually. After the race, which tends to be short and snappy – generally only a few minutes at most – you've got all the time in the world to get back up some other way, to watch how the others are doing and listen to the tall tales told by those who would have you believe they could have done better than they did.

### Uphill-Downhill

In this kind of event you first have to work up a sweat, before you get to break your bones on the way down. Separate times are generally recorded for the two sections and then totalled. Consequently, there may be three winners in any one race: the fastest rider uphill, downhill and overall. Some of these races are hardly longer in distance than the downhill, while others may take you over many miles. Generally, the organizational problems associated with many participants and long distances discourage rides over more than two miles, though they still exist and are perhaps the most exciting to participate in.

## Challenges and Enduros

A Challenge is not much more than a long uphill-downhill race or one with varied terrain. Though the route will be marked in some critical areas, you may be offered some flexibility of choice, with some daredevil always finding a new and shorter route, which may subsequently be named after him or her. Sometimes, the newly discovered shortcut becomes the established route, which may result in the same race becoming more of a challenge from year to year.

An enduro is more like the typical cyclo-cross race: many laps on a relatively compact course of perhaps one or two miles. The course will include varied terrain. Rather than overall speed, the placings at the end of each lap are recorded, with a certain numbers of points awarded to the first six riders after each lap. The point ratings are accumulated and the rider with the highest number of total points is declared the winner.

## 'Tours'

Many off-road events are billed as tours, though it can be scary to see the vehement competition that goes on there. The term is not supposed to be taken seriously by the participants: it is selected to bamboozle the authorities into giving their permission to use public lands for this kind of event. Nothing wrong about it, since there has never been a report of serious damage done on any of these tours: anybody willing to work this hard at getting anywhere fast has little time to despoil nature.

In recent years a number of these tours, such as the granddaddy of them all, the Crested Butte to Aspen ride in Colorado, had become so popular that the organizers felt obliged to discourage the competitive aspect. They arrived at a formula that seems to have the future of mountain bike participation guaranteed: a non-

Paul Hallock burning up the competition in a cloud of smoke. (Photo Donald Favello)

competitive tour with races before or afterwards. This brings together a highly motivated and knowledgeable crowd of participant-spectators for a race where the experts can measure their skills.

## Observed Trials

This is the kind of event that is highly competitive but has nothing to do with speed – the chess game of off-road biking, so to speak. It was developed mainly in the New England states and seems to trace its heritage back to motor cycling practices in those same parts of the country. The idea is to ride an impossible course without putting a foot on the ground. Bikes with very high bottom brackets, direct steering, soft tires and extremely low gears are used.

Observed trials competition is the ultimate test of skill and requires an entirely different temperament than the speed-and-thrills stuff practiced mainly in the West. Putting on an event like this is a bit of an organizational miracle, because you have to mark off the terrain accurately and you need about as many observers as you have participants. Since not too many spectators and participants can be accommodated, this kind of game will perhaps not get as much coverage as it deserves. Even so, it is definitely a fine sport – and one that can be practiced informally almost anywhere, alone or in groups.

# 12
# Mountain Bike Touring

Your mountain bike lends itself superbly to bicycle touring. By that I don't mean just any kind of riding that is not strictly for utility or sport. Though trips of several hours or so qualify as touring too, I am mainly referring here to longer rides, generally with at least one overnight stay, either all off-road or partly on regular roads. In this chapter we will look at the things to consider when bicycle touring with your mountain bike. You will find very comprehensive advice on bike touring in my *Bicycle Touring Manual*. The present chapter covers those touring aspects that are most relevant for mountain bike riders.

Mass adventure: mountain bikers camping out the night during the annual Crested Butte to Aspen mountain crossing, one of the most spectacular events on the mountain bike calendar. (David Epperson photograph)

Perhaps the best way to start out touring is gradually, finding out on shorter trips whether the whole thing appeals to you. Make sure this way that you can really handle every situation you are likely to encounter on a longer tour. Gradually progress from day rides to overnight trips to long tours. But don't forget to prepare yourself by using the bike whenever you can, running errands and commuting included. Your mountain bike is one of the most versatile machines around and can be used for all these purposes as well as for real off-road riding.

Even though you use a mountain bike, there is no need to limit your touring experience to off-road cycling. There are a number of different approaches. For instance, you may go on a longer trip along regular roads, only to take an excursion at some

point into the outback. Or you may combine a longer off-road trip with approach and return rides along the regular road. Finally, you may actually stay off-road for the entire trip, or at least a major portion of it.

Depending on your starting point and your destination, each one of these approaches to touring may be appropriate. In general, I suggest starting off without taking on really big challenges. For your first tours, select moderate distances, riding mainly on regular roads. Later you can progress to longer ones, gradually adding longer sections of off-road work. Finally proceed to real off-road tours, camping out in the wilderness for several days in a row, and carrying in food for a longer period, if needed.

### Carrying Luggage

For short tours, you can ride the bike the way it probably was when you bought it: bare. That's the way most Americans ride any bike. Personally, I prefer to install some accessories on my mountain bike, so I can handle more situations. Thus, I make sure I have lights in case my trip takes me out after dark, even if I didn't plan on it, and I mount fenders when there is the slightest chance of rain. For carrying luggage, I install at least a rack in the back and some kind of bag, even for a short trip, more for a longer one. As a permanent bag on the bike for any kind of use, I prefer a saddle bag.

The latter is a relic from my life in Britain and is highly recommended as a luggage carrying device. As illustrated in Fig. 12.1, it attaches to the saddle, which may have to be equipped with an adaptor if it doesn't have eyelets for the necessary straps. The saddle bag puts the weight of anything you carry very close to the most neutral point of the bike, thus interfering least with its handling characteristics.

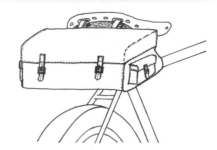

Fig. 12.1 Saddle bag

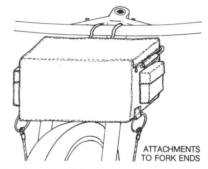

ATTACHMENTS TO FORK ENDS

Fig. 12.2 Handlebar bag

Fig. 12.3 Pannier bag attachment

The other alternatives for carrying modest amounts of luggage are the handlebar bag, a small backpack and the belt bag, more usually referred to as fanny pack in the US. Be my guest if you prefer one of these, but they are definitely less comfortable. The handlebar bag affects the bike's steering response and is of necessity modestly sized. Make sure it is at least sup-

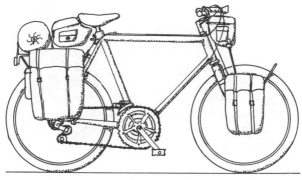

Fig. 12.4 Well-packed bike

ported by means of a bracket that keeps it in shape, supported from the top, and is restrained by means of two chook oordo running from tho bottom at either side to the tip of the front fork, as shown in Fig. 12.2. The handlebar bag is quite handy for items that require easy access along the way, including the map.

The frameless backpack has the advantage that it stays with you, even when you leave the bike somewhere. Though handlebar bags can also be equipped with carrying straps, the chances of you losing your valuables are minimized by carrying them on your body at all times. Select a model with wide and preferably padded shoulder straps and a waist strap to stop it from swaying sideways. To keep it in shape, and to protect your back from the discomfort caused by irregularly shaped items carried inside, place a piece of fiber board the size of the back panel inside the bag, or select a model with a light integral frame to serve the same purpose.

Take the right clothing and at least the essential tools and spares when touring. You may refer to Chapter 4 for como cuggoctiono on olothing and tho other absolute essentials. Even on a one-day trip, it is smart to be on the generous side. Realize that you may be riding in the cool early hours, the heat of the afternoon and in the evening. You may be far from the nearest source of food or supplies. Help may be hard to get once you are a long way from home.

For trips of several days, certainly if you are camping, quite a lot of luggage will be necessary. I suggest using pannier bags both front and rear. When packing, remember that the bike must remain stable. That means the weight must be divided relatively evenly between front and rear. In the front, the weight should be centered close to the front wheel axle, while in the back it should be as far forward as possible within the restraints of adequate heel clearance. Bags should all be attached firmly both at

Fig. 12.5 Load distribution methods

the top and pulled down and against the bike at the bottom, as shown in Fig. 12.3. A well packed machine is shown in Fig. 12.4.

Of the various ways to distribute the load, the method shown in the middle of Fig. 12.5 is the one that least affects the steering and balancing process. Make sure the racks are solidly attached to the bike and the bags are properly mounted. To test the effectiveness of your packing operation, take the loaded bike from the front by the handlebars and shake it sideways, as shown in Fig. 12.6. Sway along the axis shown there, should be minimal if it is loaded correctly.

The luggage racks themselves should be very strong and rigid. Their attachment to the bike is crucial. Special designs for mountain bike use are most suitable, since those are dimensioned to accommodate the greater clearances typical for mountain bikes. The front rack should preferably be of the so-called low rider design, shown in Fig. 12.7. The one in the rear will carry most of the weight. I suggest using pannier bags that are of modest size and complementing them with a rectangular rigid case on top of the rear luggage rack. For attachment of this case, non-stretching straps or belts are more suitable than bungees, since the former don't allow the load to shift or sway.

When it comes to packing the bags themselves, try to roll up the various items so that they form relatively long and regularly shaped packs or rolls, corresponding to the width of the bag in which they will be packed. Put the things you will need first or most suddenly at the top of the bag. This way, you don't spend a long time digging for things when you set up camp, nor will everything get wet while looking for the items to keep you dry in a storm. Maintain a certain logic, packing items that obviously belong to-

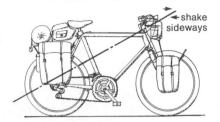

Fig. 12.6 Checking for sway

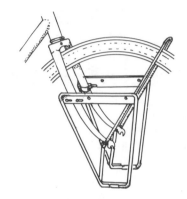

Fig. 12.7 Low-rider front rack

gether in the same bag, and small things in the outside pockets, similarly logically arranged. For more advice on packing, see my *Bicycle Touring Manual*.

### Maps and Orientation

In all touring situations, you should get familiar with the use of the map and other aids to orientation. You may get some more detailed advice on this subject from the book just mentioned. However, for most trips, it may suffice to get familiar with the map and its use. Try to visualize the situation out in the terrain before you set out, referring frequently to the map along the way, to make sure you always know where you are.

Familiarize yourself with the various characteristics of the particular map you use, including the very helpful aid to elevation provided in the form of contour lines on most Geolog-

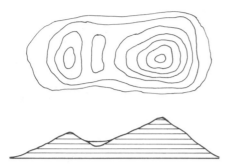

Fig. 12.8 Contour lines

ical Survey (in Britain, Ordnance Survey) maps of an acceptable scale. This, I would suggest, is about 1 : 100 000 for day rides on roads, 1 : 50 000 for real off-road work and 1 : 200 000 for longer tours of several days.

Fig. 12.8 shows the meaning of contour lines: each contour line connects all points at a certain elevation above sea level. The closer together they are, the steeper a particular route. The more you cross, the greater the overall elevation difference. If needed, also use other aids and clues to establishing the most suitable route. Even though your bike is called a mountain bike, you will probably agree that for longer trips and tours the advantage of riding on level terrain is so overwhelming, that you'll be actively in search of it as much as possible within the scope of your route.

Once you are familiar with the use of the map itself, also learn to orient yourself in the field. Remain conscious of the landmarks along the way. Consider what you see immediately along your path and what you can recognize at some distance on the horizon. Make a point of knowing when you are going in one direction or the other, whether the road continues generally up or down, or whether you are staying more or less at the same elevation. This form of orientation along the route, together with occasional consultation of the map, should help you reconstruct where you are and how you got there, so you don't even begin to get lost.

### Day Tripping

Day trips used to be the most common type of adult cycling in the US, and it is still a very rewarding pastime. Ride the bike around the countryside, have lunch along the way, and return home at night. I purposely left out one common part of the routine: loading the bikes on the car in the morning, driving out somewhere and unloading the bike, to be repeated in reverse order at the conclusion of the tour.

Mountain bike touring on rough roads in the Colorado Rockies (David Epperson/Bicycle Sport photograph)

It doesn't have to be done that way, at least not always. It's the way most hikers go about it, and for them it makes sense, since they may not ever reach reasonable hiking terrain on foot or by means of public transportation. On level ground, you move four times as fast as the hiker. Your bike is built to be conveyed on its own two wheels and few people really live so far away from suitable biking terrain that they can't start quite a number of rides from their own home.

Even if you live in the middle of a major city, you'll be surprised how quickly you get out of it on the bike. Besides, it's a real advantage not having to return to a car that's parked somewhere in the middle of nowhere, or to worry about what's happening to it while you're out riding the bike. Feel free to take the car, or some form of public transportation if you're lucky enough to live close to an operating system that takes bikes, but also consider the alternative of riding your bike all the way.

**Overnight Trips and Long Tours**

I'd say you start with tours of more than one day only after you have been on several one-day trips. Certainly the first few times, you'll be better off arranging your trip in such a way that you can spend the nights in a hotel or other reliable accommodation. Only after you have become familiar with the various problems encountered on overnight trips, should you consider camping and staying far off the beaten track.

The final stage of touring is the long tour: a ride of a week or more. Certainly if you go camping, or have to camp some nights for lack of other accommodation *en route*, prepare yourself well. Do that by first taking some overnight camping trips in more familiar terrain. As you accumulate experience, keep track of the various items you might have forgotten to account for. In fact, I consider every trip in some way a learning experience for the next one. As you gain experience and become better at it, you will enjoy touring more each time.

# 13

# The Mountain Bike for Commuting and Utility

Probably more than any other bicycle design, the mountain bike has found a use amongst utility cyclists. Their specific needs range from messenger services to shopping, commuting and running errands. Most of this mountain bike use takes place in an urban environment. Only the suburbanite commuting to his place of employ-

Typical high quality Taiwan built bike: Fisher MountainBikes' Hoo-Koo-E-Koo, named after one of the trails on Marin County's Mount Tamalpais and equipped with the kind of components that keep the price down without sacrificing quality. It seems the tires shown are a little fatter than the 1.6 inch nominal width would suggest.

ment in the city is still more likely to use a drop-handlebar derailleur machine as he is to ride a mountain bike.

In the present chapter we shall consider the various aspects of using the mountain bike for basic transportation, primarily in an urban environment. Your equipment should match the particular use. One important aspect is reliability, keeping in mind that – unlike the leisure cyclist – the utility cyclist may have to rely on his bike whatever the weather or time of day. He probably has a time schedule to meet and appointments to keep. The other important criterion is the need to carry luggage.

## Bike and Accessories

Just about any kind of mountain bike lends itself to this practical kind of use. Generally, the relatively cheap imported machines with welded frames and somewhat narrower tires are quite adequate, though you may want to use fancier equipment. Only if you live someplace where unpaved roads are common, should you have to go all the way to a genuine off-road machine with the fattest tires. Just make sure it has the requisite bosses and eyelets for the subsequent installation of accessories.

I feel any utilitarian bike should be equipped with several accessories – or at least it should be easily adaptable to be so equipped. Luggage racks, fenders, and lights should either be permanently installed or available for quick mounting. Though my own utility bike sports all of these all the time, you may prefer to just keep fenders and lights handy for installation when needed. The fenders can be held by means of home-made wing bolts, as shown in Fig. 13.1, to allow quick removal and installation.

Racks and bags for utility use are no different from those designed for touring as described in Chapter 12. What you will need more than anybody else is a lock – and you may have to use it to its full capability every time you leave the bike anywhere. To make sure the removable accessories don't get removed by the wrong people, even while the whole bike is properly locked, use a few simple tricks. As an example, you can wrap some handlebar tape around the pump and the tube against which it is installed – that is usually enough to discourage the person who wants to quickly grab it off the bike.

Don't make the removability of various items too obvious. I'd suggest avoiding quick-release hubs, since wheels with axle nuts are rarely sto-

Fig. 13.1 Fender attachment

Fig. 13.2 Three-sided luggage platform

len. To keep the saddle on the bike, you can either invest in the Hite-Rite saddle adjusting spring, or you can replace the quick-release by a regular binder bolt – after all, you probably don't have to adjust the height as often as the person who rides his mountain bike mainly up and down steep hillsides.

One home-made accessory that I find extremely handy for carrying odd items, including quite large packages, is the three-sided platform shown in Fig. 13.2. You can put any kind of item in there and restrain it adequately by means of bungees or straps. The fact that the weight is off-center seems to have little or no effect on the bike's handling characteristics. I made mine on the basis of a discarded plastic beverage crate, from which I removed two sides. It is attached to the rack by means of clips and bolts with nuts and washers. Mount it far enough to the back to clear your ankles and low enough to keep the top platform of the rack free for other items.

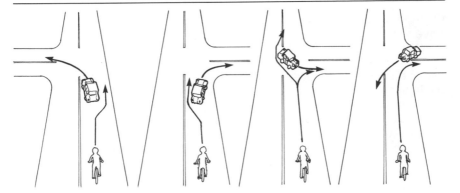

Fig. 13.3 Accident avoidance actions

## Urban Cycling

Most of your utility cycling will probably be done in an urban environment. Even if you live in a smaller community, you will find that the way to the post office and the shopping center requires riding on urban streets with relatively dense traffic. It really is not as hard as some people seem to assume.

Traffic – especially motor traffic – is not as irrational as many of my environmentally zealous friends would have us believe. It operates quite systematically and follows a predictable pattern. Many cyclists seem to have the greatest fear of motor vehicle drivers. Some motorists are indeed either reckless or out to get you. But by and large, you will find that they are a lot more predictable than pedestrians and cyclists, not to mention many of the other typical off-road hazards.

Refer to the various comments about safety, particularly regarding the risk of traffic accidents, outlined in Chapter 9. If you yourself behave sensibly and predictably, reacting logically and considerately to the actions of others, remaining always aware of the potential causes of danger, you will be able to ride in urban traffic with confidence and competence.

Cycling in dense or fast traffic is not an impossible feat, but you have to stay alert. Don't freeze up in panic, expecting the worst to happen any time. Instead, evaluate the situation consciously, and judge which dangers may be looming where. Along a straight stretch of road there is little risk of someone turning off in front of you, so you can concentrate on the scenery, relaxing a little, providing you keep an eye on the road. Though your inherent fears may tell you differently, the risk of being hit from behind is very remote if you don't suddenly divert from your position in the road. Keep a straight course, and check the road to make sure you can keep it. When you do have to divert, check behind you first.

Increase your level of attention to traffic when you approach a high-risk situation, such as a driveway with a car that may be about to enter the road. When approaching an intersection, become particularly conscious of the traffic situation. Here your choice of the correct path, as described in Chapter 9, is of utmost importance, and you have to judge what other drivers are about to do. If you misjudge the situation and have to perform a panic action to avoid a collision, use the knowledge gained in Chapter 7 and 8 about braking and diverting. Judge which way to divert, depending on the course of the 'opponent'. Fig.

13.3 gives you some examples of these actions.

If you do not at first feel at ease in these situations, start on less densely travelled streets and proceed gradually from streets and areas with relatively slow traffic to more demanding traffic patterns. All the advice given for normal situations also applies to denser or faster trafficked roads – only more so. The other side of the coin is that you should not assume you can afford to ride with disregard to others on quieter roads: though the dangers will be fewer and farther between, they must still be considered.

The advice on safe riding techniques in Chapter 9 is really all you need, providing you don't just read it, but *practice* it. It is easy enough, since it is logical. I taught my children to handle any kind of traffic, including left turns from eight-lane expressways by the time they were thirteen years old, so I figure you can probably learn to do it.

On the other hand, if you do feel a lack of confidence, don't force things either. If you can't handle that left turn, just get off the bike and cross like a pedestrian, waiting your turn to do each part. It will take you more time if you do it correctly, but it will save your nerves. Just don't try to perform some mix of vehicular and pedestrian behavior within one situation, since that is the most dangerous thing you can do.

One example of incorrect behavior that is only too common amongst novice cyclists, is riding a bike along the RH edge of the road to go straight at an intersection, and then abruptly turning left across the path of those going straight behind you. This self-inflicted danger goes way beyond anything you would risk if you acted like the driver of a vehicle, who would select the correct position in the road or within his lane well ahead of the in-

tersection, after having checked behind to ascertain there is a big enough gap between other vehicles to do so.

With your mountain bike, you have a few advantages over drivers of cars and other cyclists in urban and suburban environments. You can often choose shortcuts that are not available to the drivers of other vehicles, while your equipment is less sensitive than a regular ten-speed. Combine this possibility with that of the considerable speed you can develop, and you may turn out to make progress as fast as motorists in many situations. I know from my own experience that I got to work in San Francisco faster when commuting by bike than I could either on public transportation or by car.

## Commuting by Bike

I would suggest you progress from occasional errands by bike to using it for many of your regular transportation needs within the urban environment, and finally to commuting by bike. The latter is definitely harder, since it generally takes place in rush hour traffic. If you can get flexible working hours, you may be able to avoid the worst traffic, but the problem can't be avoided completely. Confidence comes with practice, so you can grow into your role as a competent urban cyclist.

Don't let little irritations stop you from using the bike for commuting. Cycling is at its best in nice weather, but you can also ride when it is cold or rainy, yes even in snow and ice, situations that are not entirely pleasant to handle in a car either. It is amusing to notice that in any part of the world cyclists seem to draw the line between suitable and unsuitable weather at a different point. In regions with frequent rains or cold weather, cyclists still ride their bikes – and enjoy it, even when the weather is less than optimal.

In areas like Britain, Washington State or British Columbia, where rain is the order of the day any time of the year, a little rain doesn't discourage a commuter from using his bike. On the other hand, in California experienced bicyclists hang their wheels in the willows the minute the forecast includes even the slightest chance of rain. In northern countries with frequent sub-freezing temperatures, a little frost doesn't discourage a cyclist, while in other regions anything below 60°F is regarded too cold for comfort. Just imagine how much more cycling enjoyment you can get by just raising your tolerance level to what others have to put up with habitually.

It's perfect when you have a place of work with regular safe bike storage facilities, change rooms and showers for your use. However, you can do without if you have to. When I started commuting to my city center office job with a major oil company around 1970, bicyclists were considered such an oddity that none of those facilities were available at first. In fact, bicyclists seemed to be regarded with disdain.

The 1973 oil crunch suddenly made it almost patriotic to ride a bike, and even an oil company could not get around encouraging it amongst its employees. Before that time I had neither shower nor proper storage facilities — on one occasion my bike was stolen in front of the building. Even so, I was not discouraged, habitually cycling to work long before fancy facilities became available.

If you don't get the use of a shower and change rooms, consider the obvious solution: don't cycle quite so fast that you perspire. Cycling can be just as enjoyable at 12 mph as it is at 25, and a lot more relaxing. When I grew up in Holland, everybody rode a bike to work and nobody even dreamt of taking a shower, or for that matter of being discouraged by not having one available. They simply cycled at whatever speed got them there without perspiring.

In those days few people rode their bikes specifically in order to get fit. They were fit anyway: it was merely a fringe benefit. At the lower speeds, people indeed did not gain bodily strength as much as they might by working at it harder. But they did arrive at work a lot more relaxed and displayed more long term health than today's high-strung performance freaks. Consider your priorities: if you want to live longer and be more relaxed and content, you may do fine taking it a little easier. If you prefer to exert yourself on your commute, you may consider doing the really hard work on the way home, taking it easy on the way to work.

All in all, commuting by bike is easier today than it was in the past. Bicycle commuting, as we've seen, is possible and enjoyable, even under sub-optimal conditions. Today, the circumstances are much more favorable in most jobs. If people could commute under poorer conditions, surely there should be nothing to stop you from commuting to work here and now.

# Part III
# The Mountain Bike and its Maintenance

Look, no wide handlebars
(nor special brakes or
indexed shifting and a few
other of today's popular
gadgets. This is
Bridgestone's MB1: strong,
light, agile and equipped
with the pick of
no-nonsense components.

# 14

# The Engineered Bicycle

This third part of the book is devoted mainly to the technical aspects of your mountain bike and its individual components. Not all of this may make entertaining reading for everybody. If you are satisfied using your bike the way it is, you may choose to put the book back on the shelf right here. Just remember to consult these chapters when your bike does develop a problem or If you need advice on the selection of mechanical equipment. Even so, I didn't write these chapters just for my own satisfaction: you will find lots of useful information here that can help you select and maintain your equipment more expertly.

This particular chapter will explain in some detail and in simple terms, the technical considerations that should go into the design of your bike and its components. In the remaining chapters, you will get more intimately acquainted with the various 'building blocks' that make up your bike: frame,

Still life with SunTour's top line mountain bike 'gruppo'

steering system, saddle, drivetrain, gearing mechanisms, wheels and brakes.

If you are not familiar with the various terms, refer to Fig. 2.1 in Chapter 2, which shows the complete mountain bike with its individual components labelled, to refresh your memory. The most obvious differences between the mountain bike and other derailleur machines are those that make the mountain bike more suitable for harder use on rougher terrain. These differences are not arbitrary: some real engineering thinking has gone into the design of your bike.

Relax, I shall not try to convert all readers to engineers. But I will acquaint you with the technical background that can help you determine whether your bike and its components are suitable for their use. First we shall take a look at the kind of forces to which a bicycle and its components are subjected. Following that, I shall outline some of the design criteria that allow the materials to withstand the resulting stresses.

## Static Forces and Weight

The simplest case of engineering analysis is referred to as static loading. In this form of analysis, the bike is considered standing still with the weight of the rider on it. Under these conditions the force applied to each part of the bike can be easily calculated. Dividing this force by the strength of the material used, considering an empirically determined safety factor, gives the cross section required to make the part strong enough to withstand it. Selecting a stronger material allows the part to be made with a smaller cross section, resulting in a design that is equally strong, yet lighter, assuming the two materials have the same density or specific weight.

Light weight, after all, is one of the most desirable qualities in a bicycle, providing it is not at the expense of strength. The lighter bike is more efficient, comfortable and responsive to handle. This is especially significant when it comes to accelerating and climbing, and on rough surfaces, where the lighter bike absorbs the road shock much better than the heavier one, leading to more controlled handling and less fatigue.

Another approach in coming up with a lighter design is to select a material with a lower density, such as aluminum instead of steel. Designing for the same strength, this method will only lead to a lighter construction if the chosen material is not proportionally as much weaker as it is lighter. Depending on the particular component's shape, certain aluminum alloys may or may not be used to advantage. For some parts, steel alloys may lead to lighter designs of the same strength, despite aluminum's much lower density.

## Metals and Their Alloys

Sooner or later, in any technical discourse about the bicycle, the word *alloy* is used – and is often misunderstood. Contrary to popular belief, alloy has nothing inherently to do with aluminum or light weight per se. It means nothing more than a mixture of several different metals – any metals, mixed in any ratio. Depending on the most prevalent metal in any particular mixture, you will encounter both steel and aluminum alloys. Both are of interest in bicycle design. In either case, the other elements are added in order to improve upon certain qualities of the base metal. This is one way to achieve greater strength, improved corrosion resistance, increased ductility or superior hardness.

One thing alloying does not significantly affect is density or specific weight: the various steel alloys are no lighter than pure steel. Similarly, all aluminum alloys have about the same density as ordinary pure aluminum. The lighter weight of alloy components is due to the fact that the stronger material allows the use of reduced cross sections.

In fact, alloying is only one of several ways to achieve stronger metals. Other methods used to this end include the addition of non-metallic components, heat treatment and certain procedures in the manufacturing process. Steel is no more than iron with a little carbon added. Steel gets stronger (and more easily corroded) as a higher percentage of carbon is added. Relatively strong high carbon steels are suitable for bicycle parts, and are widely used on many of the more reasonably priced bikes.

The next step in the chain of improving the properties of the material is the alloying process. Steel is often alloyed with manganese, chromium, molybdenum and vanadium, while aluminum may be alloyed with magnesium, copper and zinc. If you learn nothing else from this discourse, at least note that alloy does not mean aluminum, though a lot of bicycle components are indeed made of aluminum alloy. For bicycles and their parts, steel and aluminum alloys are both of interest.

The material properties can also be affected by the manufacturing process. This is most dramatically demonstrated by the very lightest alloy frame tubing materials. They are of interest to the builders of lightweight mountain bikes, since the rolling, drawing, and sometimes heat treating, that has gone into making these tubes, actually increases their strength to such a level that they are strong enough to be made with extremely thin walls, resulting in phenomenally light frames.

These processes have their drawbacks. The strongest tubes with their very thin walls must be handled carefully in the subsequent process of building the frame, since they may easily become so brittle as to break if they are treated at too high a temperature for some time in the frame building process. There is also a limit to decreasing the wall thickness of tubing, since it would easily be dented or may even collapse like an aluminum beverage can when the ratio between diameter and wall thickness exceeds 50 to 1.

## Joining Methods

In the construction of a bicycle frame and other tubing structures, such as forks and handlebar stems, the joints are made either by brazing or welding. In the welding process the base metal of the two parts to be joined is heated so they fuse together, while a filler metal that is similar to the base metal may be added.

Only materials of rather generous wall thickness can be welded. This process is suitable for mass-production techniques, since it can easily be automated and is suitable for both steel and aluminum tubing. When applied to high strength aluminum tubing, a subsequent heat treatment is required to return the material to its original strength. Most frame welding processes are carried out in an inert gas atmosphere, which protects against corrosion. In the description of welding processes used, such as TIG and WIG, the IG stands for this inert gas. The T stands for Tungsten and the W for Wolfram, designating the respective welding electrode material used.

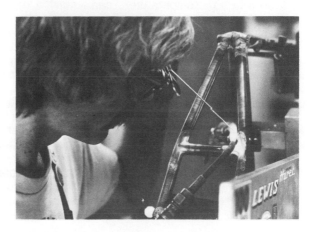

Frame builder Jeff Lindsay of Chico, California, at work, fillet brazing the seat stay bridge on one of his exclusive hand-built Mountain Goat frames.

Brazing, on the other hand, is done at much lower temperatures and is not suitable for aluminum and its alloys. In this process, the base metal is heated to a dark red first. Only then is a brazing rod with much lower melting point added, which melts between the two, forming a strong bond. It can be done with much thinner tubes than welding, but is more difficult and expensive. The nature of the metal determines how high the brazing temperature is allowed to be, and the brazing rod used must be selected to match this temperature, melting at some point well below.

Brazing rods are melted between lugs and frame tubes to join them. They comprise mainly copper, alloyed with zinc or silver and cadmium. The term *silver brazing* refers to the use of rods that are actually neither pure silver nor even predominantly silver: they merely contain *some* silver. Brazing rods with a relatively high silver content melt at lower temperatures and must therefore be used to join the most sensitive tubes of very thin, high-strength materials, which might be damaged if heated too far. Brazed joints may be made either lugged or lugless, but this nicety will be explained in Chapter 15,

Even the brazing process, despite its relatively low temperatures, can negatively affect the strength of the tubing material. As we've seen above, this applies mainly to fancy thin-walled tubes. The point affected is often not so much the area of the joint itself, but the so-called heat affected zone, some distance further along the tube. Thus it may, after one or two years of use, break at some point about ½ in to 1 in back from the joint along the tube, which just happens to be exposed to a particularly unfavorable temperature sequence during the brazing process, particularly if the frame builder heated the joint too long.

Another material that should be mentioned here is resin embedded fiber. Different varieties of this material may be used for various parts in widely different qualities. Thus, the cheapest pedals are of one variety of this material, while one of the most expensive (and as yet untested) frames is of another. When used for frames, tightly woven or matted carbon or boron fiber material, embedded in a minimum of resin, is generally selected, which is very strong and mortally expensive. Cheap parts are made with very short fibers embedded in lots of resin. One way of making cheap mass-produced frames is by means of moulding them together, forming ugly black lugs around the joints. Be prepared to see new applications of this type of material in the near future.

**Tubing Materials**

Many components of the bike, not just the frame, are constructed of tubular materials. On the outside they all look more or less the same. There are welded, plain gauge seamless and butted seamless tubes, as illustrated in Fig. 14.1. Recently, several manufacturers have introduced welded butted tubes. The differences between these various materials will be discussed in this section.

The cheapest tubes are welded. A flat plate of the thickness required for the finished tube is rolled into a tubular shape and welded up. You can tell that it's welded by feeling the welding seam or ridge inside the tube. Aluminum and steel handlebars and cheap steel frames are constructed of these materials. Nothing wrong with them, just rather heavy for any given strength, or weak if light.

More sophisticated frames are made of cold drawn welded tubes, such as those frequently used for mid-range bikes these days. The basis is a

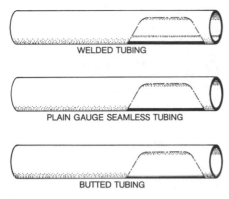

Fig. 14.1 Tubing types

welded tube of a relatively strong steel or steel alloy that is then drawn over a die to remove the weld seam and to increase its strength. Wall thicknesses tend to be less, typically around 1.0 mm, resulting in lighter structures.

On even higher quality bikes, cold drawn tubes are used. These are made by pushing a mandrel through a solid bar, and rolling it into the desired tubular shape and size. These tubes may either be plain gauge or butted. Plain gauge tubes have the same wall thickness over their entire length, while butted tubes are drawn in such a way that the ends have a greater wall thickness than the rest of the tubes. This serves both to allow for a loss of strength and to prevent damaging the tubing material where it is heated most close to the lug, as well as to accept the raised stresses at the ends of the tubes where they meet.

Recently, cold drawn welded and butted frame tubes have been introduced by several manufacturers. These are very nice materials for reasonably priced welded structures, since the butts can be made thick enough to allow welding. Let me warn you here that the term *butted* does not necessarily tell you the whole story, nor is a frame that is claimed to be made of double, triple or even quad-

ruple butted tubes necessarily better than one that is merely referred to as butted. The former terms refer to the number of wall thicknesses used somewhere along the length of the tube. The term is of course strictly incorrect, since a tube can never have more than two butts (ends).

Though most of the discussion up to this point has been based on the frame, similar considerations are applicable to the design and construction of other components, whether tubular or not. Spokes can either be plain or butted, to add strength at the point where they are stressed the most. Cranks, handlebars and rims are also shaped or reinforced to concentrate the material where it is most needed, and the welding or brazing operations explained here apply similarly to many other parts of the bike.

## Variable Forces

So far, we've only talked about the static forces. These are the forces that are applied to the bike and its components even when bike and rider are standing still or rolling along a smooth road. More important, and more complicated to predict or determine, are the variable stresses applied by a whole array of different influences. These range from the rolling of the wheels, the turning of the cranks, the torqueing effect of braking, to the jolts and blows caused by the abuse encountered when cycling off-road, not to mention what happens upon the impact of a collision.

Two aspects are of particular interest in this respect: bending stresses and fatigue. Bending stresses are of particular interest when it comes to determining the rigidity of a structure. Fatigue is of particular importance to parts that are loaded intermittently. Engineering analysis and the technology based on it make it possible to design bikes and parts so they can also withstand these effects.

To design a structure to withstand bending stresses, not only the strength of the materials, but also another property, referred to as the *modulus of elasticity*, must be taken into consideration. Whatever the strength of a material, the modulus of elasticity remains essentially the same for any given base metal. Consequently, all types of steel and its alloys, from the cheapest to the most exotic, deform equally far in response to a given bending stress, which is the quotient of force divided by cross sectional area. Similarly, all aluminum alloys deform equally, about three times as much as steel and its alloys.

There is of course a difference in reaction between a very strong metal and a weaker alloy of the same base metal. Given a certain stress, both bend equally far, but the former is more likely to spring back again when the force is released. Thus, permanent deformation is more likely with the weaker material. But we have seen that weaker materials should be made of greater wall thickness, so they don't bend as much, eliminating the risk of permanent deformation if properly designed.

The temporary or *elastic* deformation, which makes a bike or a part less rigid, is therefore greater for a sophisticated component made of a strong alloy, due to the smaller cross section used. Since rigidity is actually a desirable quality, which affects how well a bike tracks and how precisely it handles, there is a certain incongruity here. Essentially, the cheaper bike is more rigid than the fancy light bike made of the strongest materials. Fig. 14.2 illustrates these effects in the case of a simple rectangular cross section, while Fig. 14.3 shows what effect there is in the case of tubular cross sections.

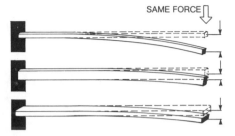

Fig. 14.2 The factors affecting rigidity

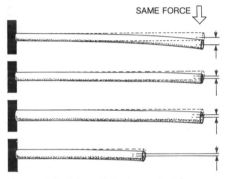

Fig. 14.3 Rigidity of tubular materials

As you can see from these illustrations, there are two ways to make a part of a given material and cross section more rigid, resulting in less deformation: either a larger tube diameter (even if the total amount of metal in the cross section remains the same) or a shorter member will do the trick. Both methods have been put into practice in mountain bike design for higher quality machines, which need as much rigidity as their thin-walled materials will allow.

The advantage of the shorter member accounts for the tendency to design components – ranging from whole frames to minor items such as cantilever brake parts – with minimal clearances, so they can be kept short and light. Larger diameters consistent with a moderate wall thickness are applied in the design of all mountain bikes. This will be evident when comparing their tube diameters with those

For the same rigidity, aluminum tubes must be either much thicker or of slightly greater tube diameter.

STEEL    ALUMINUM    ALUMINUM
         (THICK WALL)    (LARGE DIA.)

Fig. 14.4 Rigidity and strength of steel and aluminum

used on other types of bikes: they are greater than those used for ten-speeds.

Due to its much lower modulus of elasticity, aluminum frames and components are potentially less rigid, making them particularly sensitive to these restraints. Fig. 14.4 compares typical dimensions of alloy steel and aluminum tubes resulting in similar strength and rigidity. The increased tube diameter is very much in evidence on high quality aluminum

Cannondale's welded aluminum frame mountain bike. Notice the oversize frame tubes. With its very high bottom bracket and a 24 inch rear wheel, this may be a great bike for observed trials competition.

frames, such as those built by Gary Klein, Charlie Cunningham, and even the mass-produced bikes, such as those made by Cannondale and an increasing number of other manufacturers.

## Fatigue

Many parts of the bicycle are exposed to ever changing loads, usually in a cyclical pattern. This can lead to fatigue failure if the parts are not designed with this kind of loading in mind. Though the design may be quite adequate to take the highest static force ever encountered, it may fail suddenly after it has gone through many stress cycles. Thus, spokes and even frame tubes may suddenly break after a certain number of miles of use.

The designer must know what are the fatigue properties of the material selected and apply an appropriate safety factor to compensate for them. In addition, so-called stress raisers must be avoided. Stress raisers are points that are particularly prone to fatigue failure due to their geometry. In practice, they occur at every point

where a cyclically loaded part has an abrupt change of cross section or a sharp bend or corner. Look for smooth contours on such heavily stressed parts on the bike to minimize the risk of fatigue failure.

### Moving Parts

Many parts of the bike move relative to one another. Those that do so cyclically during the course of the ride are generally referred to as moving parts. All have some kind of bearings, either in the form of two sliding surfaces, such as in the various parts of the chain, or in the form of a ball bearing. To minimize friction, the quality and the lubrication of the various bearings are critically important.

The bearing surfaces should not only be smooth and perfectly round and aligned, they must also be extremely hard, if wear and the resulting friction are to be minimized. On high quality bikes and components, the various bearing parts are made of hardened steel that is subsequently ground and polished, resulting in smooth running and low wear.

Most of the critical bearings on the bike are in the form of ball bearings, consisting of an inner race and an outer race that are separated by perfectly matching ball bearings, floating in lubricant. The typical bicycle ball bearing is the adjustable cup-and-cone model illustrated in Fig. 14.5. When properly maintained, this is still the ultimate bearing, offering the best qualities for its weight. It is adjusted by turning the cone (or in some cases the cup) relative to the other part, so the gap between the two, where the bearings balls lie, is closed up a little. The lubricant should preferably be oil, though grease is more commonly used, being packed in only once or twice a year, whereas oil must be replenished frequently.

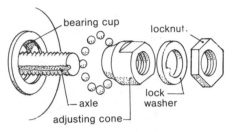

Fig. 14.5 Adjustable ball bearing

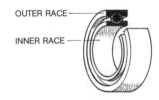

Fig. 14.6 Cartridge bearing

One problem with this kind of bearing is that it is not perfectly sealed against the elements. A better seal can generally be used on Conrad or cartridge bearings, which are the common industrial type, illustrated in Fig. 14.6. These are not adjustable and generally incorrectly referred to as sealed bearings. They are generally lubricated for life – though that may actually be shorter than it is for a corresponding cup-and-cone model. When this kind of bearing becomes loose or develops increased friction, it must be replaced in its entirety, which can generally only be done by a bike mechanic, using special tools for the job.

### Screw Threads

Many of the bicycle's bits and pieces are held together by means of threaded connections, shown in Fig. 14.7. Each of these consists of a part with an exterior or *male* thread that fits inside one with an interior or *female* thread. Each of the threads is a helical groove, spiralling around the circumference. Obviously, the two threads of

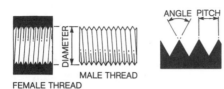

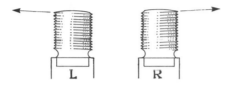

Fig. 14.7 Screw thread

Fig. 14.8 RH and LH screw thread

matching parts must have the same thread profile and the same nominal diameter, measured as the outside diameter of the male part.

The thread profile is defined by the distance between one groove or ridge and the next and the shape of the thread, referred to as pitch and thread angle, respectively. The pitch is either defined in mm as the actual distance between two ridges, or as the number of threads per inch, depending whether we are talking about metric or English threading. Though the thread angle can also vary (either 60°or 55°), this characteristic is rarely quoted on parts. Always make sure you get parts that match perfectly, which in some cases means you have to replace both parts of a connection when only one is worn or damaged – ask at a bike shop to make sure you get the right matching parts.

On bicycles, some parts are held on with LH thread, while all regular bolts and nuts, as well as most other parts, rely on RH thread. While the normal RH threading must be turned to the right to tighten, and to the left to loosen, it's the other way round for LH threading. LH threaded parts on your bike are the LH pedal-to-crank connection, shown in Fig. 14.8, and some of the guts inside your freewheel.

The correct treatment of threaded parts includes making sure they are kept clean, slightly lubricated and un-damaged. To loosen or tighten a threaded joint, always use tools with adequate leverage that fit exactly. Use wrenches for the bolts, flat screwdrivers for ordinary screws, Allen keys for the type with a hexagonal recess, Phillips head screw drivers for the type with a cross-pattern head. Wherever possible, place a plain washer under the nut or the bolt head (whichever is the part that will be turned to tighten or loosen), so contact friction is minimized, to assure the best hold between the threaded parts.

The engineered crankset, designed and built by the Cook Brothers, former BMX riders and builders, who also became pioneers in the design of mountain bike equipment – and very strong riders.

### Finishing Processes

Even the finish applied to the bicycle's various components has a technical significance. Not only is it intended to keep the bike looking pretty, it also protects the underlying material. In some cases the finishing process actually improves the characteristics of the materials. An example of this is the anodizing process used on many aluminum parts, such as the chainwheels and the rims. If applied to a depth of 0.05 mm, rather than the usual 0.005 mm typical for mere corrosion protection, it actually hardens the material in that area enough to increase the part's wear resistance properties. Parts treated this way may look dull grey, and are often incorrectly referred to as heat treated. That may or may not be the case, but generally, the appearance and any hardness advantage are due merely to the deep anodization.

Anodizing is an electro-chemical oxidation process, turning the outer layer of aluminum into a much harder form of aluminum oxide. In some circles it is popular to mix a colored die in with the anodizing bath to achieve a metallic colored finish. Even to those who think this looks nice in the showroom, it becomes pretty ugly after a while, since the slightest wear or damage shows up as an ugly discoloration – unavoidable in places like the sides of the rims, where the brake blocks wear through the finish in no time.

Bright, shiny parts that are not made of aluminum are probably of chrome plated steel. The prettiest and most durable chrome plating finishes consist of at least a layer of nickel plating, covered by a layer of chrome plating. Since the nickel is softer, it follows the contours of the material better, even if it is deformed, whereas chrome may peel off when deformed. For that reason, bolts and spoke nipples are better left just nickel plated. Zinc and cadmium are other materials that may be applied to prevent corrosion, being somewhat dull grey, but just as durable. Treat all unpainted finishes like these with a cloth and some vaseline from time to time to protect them.

Paint finishes for mountain bikes have gone through a veritable revolution since the machine was first introduced. Whereas the first models invariably had dull and earthy colors, the brightest, poppiest colors seem barely wild enough these days. Good paint is hard paint, whatever make, color or type is used, and it should cover the bike right up to the tiniest nooks and crannies.

# 15
# The Frame

The bike's frame could be called its backbone – the structure that holds it all together. Though the frame on a mountain bike at first looks like that on any other bicycle, it does differ on a number of points, in order to accommodate the particular kind of use and abuse for which it is intended. In this chapter we shall look at what all bicycle frames have in common, and at what is so special about the frame of a mountain bike.

Fig. 15.1 shows the components that constitute the mountain bike frame. The main frame comprises four relatively large diameter tubes: top tube, seat tube, down tube and head tube. The rear triangle consists of two seat stays and two chain stays. The smaller members are the bottom bracket, seat lug, upper and lower

Bridgestone's MB1. Drop handlebars, 72 degree frame angles, cantilever brakes and round chainwheels.

head lugs, assuming the bike has a lugged frame, and bridge pieces connecting the pairs of seat stays and chain stays. Finally, there are drop-outs and a number of braze-ons. The latter are minor items attached to the tubes, such as brake pivots, cable anchors, stops, bosses and guides.

As explained in Chapter 14, there are at least three ways to make a frame, illustrated in Fig. 15.2. Conventionally, quality bike frames have been made by brazing the tubes together with lugs. It is also possible to braze the tubes together directly, referred to as lugless brazing. Finally, they may be welded.

The welding process commonly used is referred to as TIG welding, which was explained in Chapter 14. The lugless joints of a TIG-welded frame are markedly more abrupt than they are on a lugless brazed frame, except if the contours are hidden by

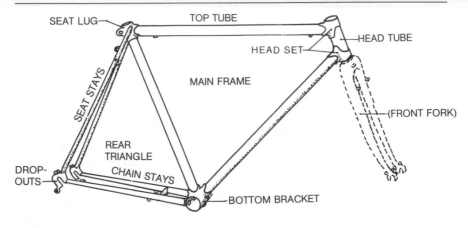

Fig. 15.1 The parts of the frame

means of a polyester spackling com-
pound. TIG-welding is cheaper than
brazing but works very satisfactorily
on tubes with slightly thicker ends. All
three methods can result in equally
strong and reliable frames.

### Judging Frame Quality

To size up the quality of a mountain
bike frame quickly, note the diameters
of the various tubes. At least the down
tube should be about ⅛ in (3 mm)
thicker than the one used on a regular
road bicycle of the same material.
This is necessary to accommodate
the higher stresses resulting from the
rougher treatment and the more
generous lengths, slopes and clearances of the mountain bike.

   Also observe the other details. If the
joints are smooth and without gaps,
whether lugged or not, the bike is
probably of a higher quality than if
they are rough and show gaps between the various parts. Finally, note
the paint finish: a good, hard, smooth
coat of paint generally indicates a
more carefully built machine. Just the
same, it is dangerous to judge a book
by its cover, or a frame by its color. I
know of at least one superb aluminum
frame that is not painted at all.

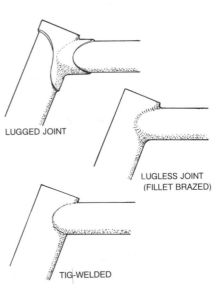

Fig. 15.2 Frame joining methods

### Frame Geometry

Fig. 15.3 compares the geometries of
a typical mountain bike and a typical
regular derailleur bike for the same
size rider. The differences can be
summarized in the following list and
will be further explained below:

☐ The mountain bike has a higher bottom bracket, despite its slightly
   smaller wheels.

Fig. 15.3 Frame geometry comparison

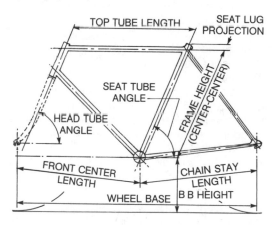

Fig. 15.4 Frame angles and dimensions

☐ For the same size rider, the mountain bike's top tube is lower. This, in addition to the higher bottom bracket results in a considerably shorter seat tube.

☐ Though the seat tube angle should be roughly the same, the mountain bike has a shallower head tube angle.

☐ The top tube tends to be slightly longer on a mountain bike.

☐ The mountain bike has longer chain stays.

☐ The last three points add up to a significantly longer total wheel base, which is the distance between the wheel axles.

☐ Though not visible here, the clearances for the wheels are more generous on the mountain bike, both radially and laterally.

Fig. 15.4 illustrates the various dimensions and angles, while the following paragraphs offer explanations for the differences and criteria for the selection of an optimum frame geometry. Most manufacturers nowadays include drawings showing the geometries of their various models in their catalogs, so you can shop around. Just the same, don't buy a bike without having tried it out, even if the geometry seems perfect on paper: the proof of the pudding is in the eating.

The bottom bracket is typically 12 in (30 cm) or more off the ground, which is at least an inch more than on a road bike. This greater height is required to provide adequate ground clearance in rough terrain, particularly in view of the mountain bike's longer wheel base, and to prevent damage to the chainwheel. Even higher bottom brackets make a bike more suitable for extremely rough terrain, such as encountered in observed trials competition.

The top tube is lower to allow a low enough saddle position that makes it possible to reach the ground while seated, and to let you straddle the bike more easily when you are standing still. In general, it should be at least two inches lower than on a tenspeed bike for the same rider. The combined effect of the higher bottom bracket with that of the lower top tube, should result in a seat tube length or frame size that is about 3 in (7.5 cm) less than it would be for a regular tenspeed. If you can't straddle the frame of a bike with wheels installed, with both feet flat on the ground and at least two inches of crotch clearance, the frame is too big.

Table 1 in the Appendix shows recommended seat tube lengths, measured one of two different ways, as well as straddle heights. In the English speaking world, bike frames used to be measured as the length from the center of the bottom bracket to the top of the seat lug. The more sensible method of measuring between the center of the bottom bracket and the centerline of the top tube is rapidly becoming universally used for mountain bike frame size designation. Some manufacturers now also refer to the straddling height, or the height of the top of the top tube above the ground.

The seat tube angle merely determines how the seat will be centered relative to the drivetrain. With the common bicycle geometry, 73° is just about right – whether mountain bike or not. This angle allows you to get up from the saddle to apply the force of your weight to the pedals quite readily, while keeping your weight reasonably balanced between front and rear

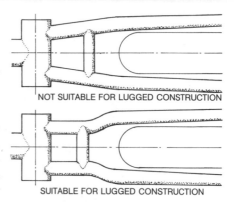

NOT SUITABLE FOR LUGGED CONSTRUCTION

SUITABLE FOR LUGGED CONSTRUCTION

Fig. 15.5 Rear wheel clearance

wheels when seated.

The head tube angle influences the steering characteristics, the overall wheelbase and the comfort or springiness of the front end. To this end, any angle between 68° and 72° may be right. It may be as shallow as 68° for a sluggish but comfortable bike that goes downhill without risk and is suitable for the less accomplished rider. It should be more like 72° for a bike that gives a nimbler, though rougher, ride – one that demands more skill on a steep descent.

The longer top tube has two functions. It protects your knees when standing up on a steep climb and provides an acceptably long wheelbase. My experience indicates that bikes with shorter top tubes for any given frame size tend to be more enjoyable to ride. About 2–3 in more than the seat tube length (measured center-to-center) is about right for most riders. If you still hit your knee caps when grinding uphill, you should get a handlebar stem with more reach, rather than a longer top tube.

The longer chain stays provide the greater clearances and contribute to the longer wheelbase. Generally, relatively short chain stays and the resulting shorter wheelbase provide better climbing and sprinting characteris-

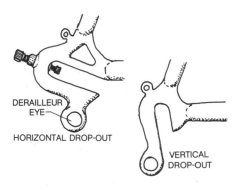

DERAILLEUR
EYE

HORIZONTAL DROP-OUT

VERTICAL
DROP-OUT

Fig. 15.6 Drop-outs

tics. I'd say anything less than 17 in (430 mm) chain stays, usually resulting in less than 43 in (100 cm) wheelbase) provides a nimbler ride. The frame of a mountain bike intended for the novice should probably be longer than that.

There are various ways to give the mountain bike frame the lateral clearance around the wheels to accommodate the fattest tires, as shown in Fig. 15.5. You need at least ³⁄₁₆ in (5 mm) lateral clearance on either side. Some bikes just don't take the really fat tires. This is not necessarily bad, though I'd prefer one that can be used with any size tire – up to the full width of 2.2 in (59 mm). Measure the distance between the pairs of chain and seat stays at a point 13 inches from the drop-out centers; then deduct ³⁄₈ in (10 mm) to determine which is the fattest tire that will fit with adequate clearance.

**Frame Materials**

You may want to refer to Chapter 14 again, where we have looked at the various materials and their properties. There are many ways of achieving a frame of adequate quality. The fanciest ones are either made of butted tubes, brazed together lugless, also referred to as fillet brazed, or of

welded and stress relieved aluminum. The first satisfactory mountain bikes were all made without lugs, since at that time none were available to fit the larger diameter tubes needed for a reliable mountain bike. There are now lugs available to fit the large diameter mountain bike tubes, and many excellent lower price mountain bikes are constructed this way.

I find the use of TIG-welded frames of slightly thicker butted materials quite adequate, providing high strength alloy steel tubes are used with a wall thickness of no more than 0.8 mm in the center section. Anything thicker and heavier seems to result in a rather harsh and less nimble ride, even though the difference in weight is only on the order of one or two pounds in all. Any tubing referred to as HiTen, or some similar term, is merely carbon steel. These are of necessity either heavier or weaker, on account of the material's inferior strength as compared to most steel alloys.

Clever way to get the rear wheel centered to avoid unequal spoke tension: the LH drop-out is offset to the inside on this frame by Hans Mittendorf,

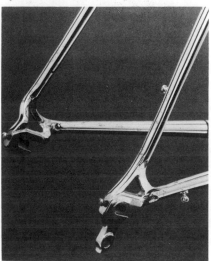

The type of tubing used is generally acknowledged by a sticker, generally attached to the seat tube, especially if it is tubing of recognized quality. Table 15-I summarizes the dimensions of a number of steel frame tubing materials, compared to the dimensions of typical frame tubes for a regular 10-speed derailleur bike. Aluminum tubing is not included in this summary, as it varies too much from one make to the other. It should be made of even greater diameters and wall thicknesses than steel tubes, to be adequately rigid and strong, respectively.

### Frame Details

In addition to the materials and the geometry, several less obvious points affect the quality of your frame. First, the drop-outs are of some importance. These are the flat parts where the rear wheel is installed, shown in Fig. 15.6. They should be relatively thick and rounded, indicating that they are made of either forged or investment cast steel. These are superior in strength and, due to the greater thickness, in rigidity to the type made of flat stamped steel plate. Aluminum drop-outs had better be really thick, to the point of being ugly.

The slot for the rear wheel in the drop-outs may be either vertical or horizontal. The former method allows closer clearances between the wheel and the chain stay bridge, resulting in a more rigid rear end and a more constant brake position relative to the rim. Since the wheel can not be adjusted by pushing it forward more on one side than on the other, this kind of drop-out requires a greater degree of precision in building the frame. Check from behind, looking along both wheels, to make sure the two wheels track, meaning they are perfectly aligned, when the axle is at the top of the slot on both sides.

**Table 15.I Examples of frame tubing dimensions (all dimensions in mm)**

| Tube | Mountain Bike tubing (typical examples) outside dia. and (wall thickness) | | | | Conventional tubing outside diameter |
|---|---|---|---|---|---|
| | Tange Prestige MTB | Tange MTB | Ishiwata MTB D | Reynolds 531 ATB | |
| Top tube | 28.6 (1.0/0.7) | 28.6 (1.2/0.9) | 28.6 (1.0/0.9) | 28.6 (0.9/0.6) | 25.4 |
| Down tube | 31.8 (0.9/0.6) | 31.8 1.2/0.9) | 31.8 (1.2/0.9) | 31.7 (1.02) | 28.6 |
| Seat tube | 28.6 (1.2/0.6) | 28.6 (1.2/0.9) | 28.6 (1.2/0.9) | 28.6 (0.8/0.55) | 28.6 |
| Head tube | 31.8 (1.0) | 33.0 (1.5) | 33.0 (1.5) | 31.7 (0.9) | 31.7 |
| Chain stay | 22.2/13 (0.8) | 22.2/13 (1.0) | 28/20 (1.0) | 22.2 (1.2) | 22.2/12.5 |
| Seat stay | 15.9/11 (0.6) | 15.9/11 (1.0) | 16 (1.0) | 16 (0.9) | 11/14/12 |
| Fork blade | 25.4/13 (1.1) | 25.4/13 (1.1) | 25.4/14 (1.2) | 29.8 x 19.8 (0.9) | 27.5 x 20/12.5 |
| Steerer | 25.4 (2.5/1.6) | 25.4 (2.6/1.6) | 25.4 (1.2) | 25.4 (2.3/1.6) | 25.4 |

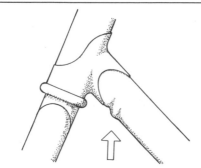

Fig. 15.7 Downtube damage

There must be a derailleur eye on the RH drop-out. It should be as thick as the rest of the drop-out, to make sure it does not get bent, resulting in derailleur misalignment and consequently in unpredictable gear changing. Since various derailleurs are designed differently, make sure the two match when you have to replace the derailleur.

The bridges between the chain stays and the seat stays should be attached with perfectly smooth and uninterrupted welds or brazed joints. The same goes for the various other braze-ons, which should include the following:

☐ Pivot bosses for the rear brake, generally installed below the chain stays these days, except for cantilever brakes, which have them on the seat stays. Though there is a certain degree of standardization between various makes, check when replacing brakes that they match the bosses on the frame by inquiring about interchangeability at a bike shop.
☐ A rigid anchor for the end of the outer brake cable. To accommodate a cantilever brake, it must be in the form of a tubular bridge between the rear stays with a tunnel or recess in which the cable end is restrained. Roller-cam and U-brakes, which are generally installed below the chain stays, would need a solid

lug below the bottom bracket or on the bottom of the down tube just ahead of the bottom bracket.
☐ Guides or tunnels for the brake and gear cables, including stops at those points where outer cable sections are interrupted.
☐ Threaded eyelets and lugs for the installation of a luggage rack and fenders, as well as a hole in the bridge between the seat stays to mount fenders. Even if you don't want to think about such accessories right now, it doesn't hurt to know you can accommodate them if necessary.
☐ Threaded bosses for the installation of water bottles. Generally, three locations are suitable: the front of the seat tube, the top of the down tube, and below the down tube. Your bike will be most versatile if you have all three, so you still have enough bottle carrying options after you install a lock and a pump.
☐ One or more pegs or anchors for the pump, which can be either clamped between two pegs or between one peg and some corner of the frame. A nice place is along the rear side of the seat tube, if the chain stays are long enough to provide adequate clearance there, leaving the front of the seat tube free for your lock.

**Frame Maintenance**
Even the mountain bike frame is not indestructible. If it gets seriously damaged, take it to a bike shop to evaluate the possibility of repair, rather than replacing the frame or the entire bike. However, some checks and repairs can be carried out by the technically inclined layman, which will be covered in this section.

The most important thing to know is how you can judge whether anything is wrong with the frame. This should

Pull wire taut – distance between wire and seat tube must measure the same on both sides

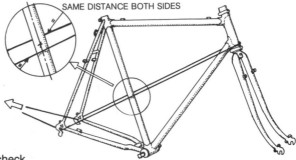
SAME DISTANCE BOTH SIDES

Fig. 15.8 Frame alignment check

be done after a serious crash and whenever you get the feeling the bike is not tracking as well as it used to.

The weak point on the frame is the forward section of the down tube, just behind the lower head lug. After a collision, check to make sure there is no bulge or wrinkle at this point, as illustrated in Fig. 15.7. If there is, take the bike to the shop for advice. On a high quality machine, it is quite realistic to get a frame builder to replace the down tube in a case like this.

Other kinds of damage to the frame more typically result in a lateral misalignment. For a simple check, wrap a piece of string around the head tube and the drop-outs, as shown in Fig. 15.8. Pull taut and measure the distance between string and seat tube, comparing it both sides. If the difference is more than about 2 mm (3/32 in), the bike will bear some aligning,

which can be done on all but the most fragile machines. Once more, this is a job for an experienced bike mechanic.

What you can do yourself, is touch up the paint when it gets scratched. Get a bottle of touch-up paint of the right color at the time you buy the bike, since the color choice seems to differ from year to year, and this year's colors may not be stocked next year. Sand the spot down to bare metal, then clean with turpentine or paint thinner. Apply paint with a very small brush with short bristles, avoiding overlapping over the undamaged paint. If you can only get touch-up paint in a spray bottle, spray a little puddle in a metal bottle cap or similar small receptacle and apply it with a brush. Clean the brush with turpentine or paint thinner afterwards. Let the paint dry overnight and repeat the application if necessary.

# 16
# The Steering System

The mountain bike's steering system is depicted in Fig. 16.1. It comprises front fork, upper and lower headset bearings, stem and handlebars. Each of these items differs somewhat from the corresponding parts installed on other bikes, since your mountain bike's front end is subjected to particularly punishing use and is crucial for the way the machine handles.

### Handling Characteristics and Steering Geometry

The bicycle is not steered merely by turning the handlebars. In fact, given a reasonably constant road surface, it can be steered successfully without ever touching the handlebars. You

Nowadays, almost all mountain bikes have a steering system with a unicrown fork, relatively narrow bars and a stem with a single clamp, like this Fisher bike.

can get a good feel for the bike's handling by walking it, held only at the saddle. Lean the bike one way or the other, and it turns towards that same direction. Bring it back upright, and it will straighten out again.

The position of the steering system changes in response to the lean. At a given speed, a particular lean will point the front wheel under a certain angle. Going faster, a more pronounced lean is required to achieve the same curve radius. Going slower, quite a small amount of lean is enough to turn quite abruptly. Standing still, the bike is 'rudderless', unless the handlebars are held.

The cyclist has to hold the handlebars for only two reasons: to guide the bike when standing still or riding very slowly, and to dampen the effect of extraneous influences, such as sur-

face unevenness, which would otherwise upset the balance, pushing the front wheel off its course. Such an extraneous force could divert the wheel far enough to lead to a diverting type fall, as explained in Chapter 9.

What keeps the bike following its own course at some speed, is known as trail, the most significant element of steering geometry. Steering geometry is the entire interrelationship of angles and dimensions of the steering system. Trail is depicted in Fig. 16.2: it is the horizontal distance between the point where the front wheel contacts the ground and the point where a line through the steering axis touches the ground.

All bicycles have positive trail, meaning that the line through the steering axis intersects the road at some point *in front* of the contact point between the tire and the road. The bike would be virtually unsteerable if it were the other way round. The amount of trail essentially determines the stability and self-steering characteristics of the bike. On the other hand, too much trail makes the bike sluggish to handle, so it becomes a matter of fine tuning.

These characteristics also depend on the angle between the steering axis and the horizontal plane. For any steering angle, a particular amount of trail results in a certain stability. With a given steering angle, the trail can be varied by selecting the fork design appropriately. This is achieved by selecting one with more or less fork rake. The rake is the distance by which the fork blades are bent forward. You'll probably never get a chance to select any of this: the manufacturer takes care of that.

To obtain the kind of handling that agrees with off-road cycling, the mountain bike should have more trail than a road bike. This increases the bicycle's tendency to go straight, re-

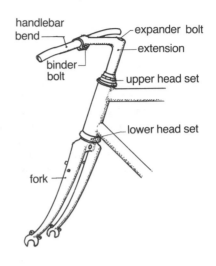

Fig. 16.1 The steering system

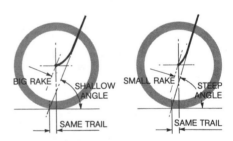

Fig. 16.2 Steering system trail

quiring less force to keep it on course when the front wheel is diverted by irregularities in the surface. The granddaddy of today's mountain bike, the Schwinn Excelsior, had a 68° head angle and a two inch fork rake, resulting in a trail of 80 mm (3¼ in). There probably isn't a better configuration for downhill riding.

However, unlike the California prototypes of the late seventies and early eighties, most of today's mountain bikes are used for lots of other things, and those that are ridden down steep hillsides are often steered by highly skilled bicycle acrobats. Consequently, different designs are showing up more and more. The range of head angles varies from about 67° to

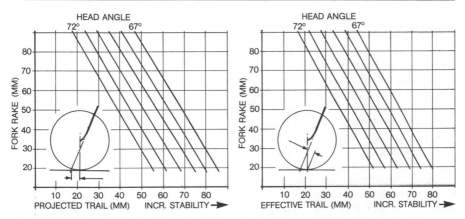

Fig. 16.3 Trail and effective trail, as affected by steering angle and fork rake

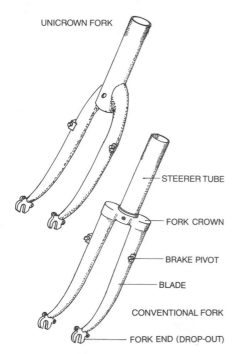

Fig. 16.4 Fork types

72°, with rakes that differ enough to make one bike a sure descender, a second a nimble climber and another a stable low-speed trials machine.

Fig. 16.3 summarizes the effect of various combinations of steering angle and fork rake, showing two dif-ferent varieties of trail. The first is what I refer to as simple or projected trail, the other one is what I call *effective trail*. The latter measure, derived in the RH graph, is the more accurate one, taking into account the effect of the angle under which trail and rake are measured relative to each other as a function of the steering angle. The effective trail is what has been re-ferred to by some authors as the *sta-bility index*. Though the difference be-tween projected and effective trail are minor, it increases as head angles di-verge more, accounting for the dramatic difference in handling characteristics between two bikes with identical trail, but different head angles.

### The Front Fork

In the following sections, I shall de-scribe the various parts of the steering system, starting here with the front fork. This component also serves as an effective suspension system for the mountain bike, elastically absorb-ing shocks. This shock absorption property is greatest when the head angle is small and the rake corres-pondingly long. On the other hand, this also results in a weaker front end, given the same materials and wall thicknesses, as well as making the bike a little sluggish.

Two basic fork designs are used for mountain bikes, as illustrated in Fig. 16.4. Both types have a steerer tube (steering column in Britain), two fork blades and fork ends. In addition, the traditional front fork, used almost exclusively on non-mountain bikes, has a separate cast, forged or pressed fork crown, into which the blades are installed. Most mountain bikes these days use a fork of the *unicrown* design, on which the fork blades are bent inward near the top and welded to the steerer tube. After bending several forks with separate crowns on my mountain bike, I swear by the unicrown solution. A variation of this type of fork, pioneered by Charlie Cunningham on some of his aluminum bikes, does away with the forward curve of blades, which are instead installed under an angle relative to the front axle to achieve the same rake.

Though unicrowns are currently the favored design, not all are equal. Some manufacturers take shortcuts, and many cheaper bikes come with unicrown forks that are not adequately reinforced. If the fork blades are made of butted tubing with significantly greater wall thickness near the top than elsewhere, the unicrown design works fine. If not, an additional reinforcing piece should have been brazed over the top of the curved section.

On the mountain bike, the fork's steerer tube has the same diameter and threading as used on ten-speeds. Actually, several types of threading standards exist, but all mountain bike makers adhere to British bicycle industry standard dimensions, which includes 1.000 in x 24 tpi screw thread. The inside diameter must also be the same as used on regular bikes built to English standard dimensions, at least near the top, so the handlebar stem

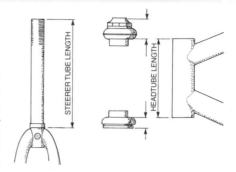

Fig. 16.5 Steerer tube length determination

can be inserted. The stem length must match the size of the bike's head tube.

On the fork blades, pivot bosses must be installed to accept the cantilever or roller-cam brakes used on the mountain bike. They should be in the appropriate location and of the right type to match the particular make and model of brake used. Though a brake bolt mounting hole, as required on a regular road bike with caliper brakes, is not strictly needed, either a normal hole or a threaded one comes in handy to mount fenders or a rack.

The fork ends should be just about as thick as rear drop-outs, and investment cast or forged models are much stronger than those made of stamped plate. If the bike is not intended primarily for racing, I'd make sure the fork ends have threaded eyelets for rack or fender mounting. In addition, threaded bosses should be brazed on to the fork blades to install a rack. Bikes sold in Britain should preferably have a threaded boss to mount a lamp bracket for the front light. I think that would make sense elsewhere too, but both the British battery lights and the matching lamp brackets are virtually unknown elsewhere.

### Fork Maintenance

The fork is the most likely component to get serious damage when you hit

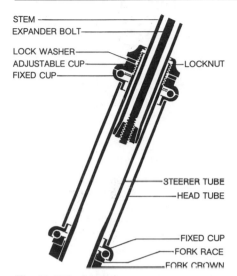

Fig. 16.6 The headset

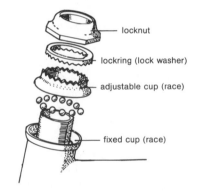

Fig. 16.7 Headset adjusting parts

an obstacle head-on. If there is no evidence of cracks or folds it may be possible to have it straightened at a bike shop. If the problem is more serious, replace the fork, which you can do yourself. Remove the handlebars and undo the headset as explained below. Take the old fork to the shop to order a replacement of the same size. If they don't have your size, get one with a longer steerer tube and cut it to size with a hacksaw. Make sure the threaded section is long enough to install the upper head-set, being about 3 cm (1¼ in). The bike shop can cut

the thread further if necessary. Fig. 16.5 shows how to determine the right length if you don't have the old one handy: add the headset's so-called stacking height to the length of your frame's head tube and deduct 2 mm (a little over ¹⁄₁₆ in) for clearance.

If the steering does not turn freely, and adjusting the headset, as described below, does not do the trick, it may be due to a bent steerer tube. In that case the fork must be replaced. Whenever replacing, removing or reinstalling a front fork, heed the advice contained in the section about headset maintenance below.

### The Headset

Depending on the inside diameter of the head tube, your mountain bike may either have a standard headset or the larger diameter model used on many BMX bikes. Both are built up similarly, as illustrated in Fig. 16.6. Some models have an additional locking device to stop the locknut from coming loose under the effect of vibrations.

The fixed bearing races are dished and are installed with a compression fit inside the top and bottom of the head tube, respectively. The bearing balls lie in these races, which should be packed with clean bearing grease at least once a season. The bearing balls may either be loose or contained in a retainer. The fork race is pushed on a shoulder at the bottom of the steerer tube. Several different sizes are in use, so make sure you get the right size when replacing it.

### Headset Adjustment

When the steering is either loose or rough, try to solve your problem by adjusting the headset first. The entire headset is adjusted from the top, as shown in Fig. 16.7. All you need is a large adjustable wrench and a rag, proceeding as follows:

1. Undo the locknut on top (after loosening the special locking insert screw that is installed on a few models).
2. Raise the lock washer underneath the locknut.
3. Turn the adjusting cup to the right to tighten, the left to loosen.
4. When it feels right – no play in the bearing, yet turning smoothly – tighten the locknut, while holding the adjusting cup in place.
5. Try again. If necessary, repeat and loosen or tighten a little, perhaps ⅛ of a turn.

**Overhaul or Replace Headset**

Overhaul the entire headset if adjusting does not solve the problem. The same procedure must be followed when replacing either the fork or the headset. Before you start, remove the handlebars, as described in the appropriate section below, and the front wheel, as explained in Chapter 20. You need a large adjustable or special wrench and a rag. If you have to replace the fixed cups and the fork race, rely on your bike shop for this part of the project, since it is best done with special removal and installation tools. If you insist on doing it yourself, refer to my *Bicycle Repair Book* for instructions based on the use of improvised tools.

*Disassembly procedure:*
1. Unscrew and remove the locknut.
2. Remove the lock washer.
3. Unscrew and remove the adjusting race, holding the fork in the frame at the bottom.
4. Catch the ball bearings, which are best replaced together with their retainer each time you overhaul a headset.
5. Remove the fork from the head tube, catching the bearings on the other side similarly.

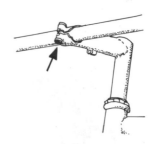

Fig. 16.8 Adjustable stem and handlebars

6. Inspect all parts. Replace any parts that are obviously worn, corroded or damaged. This will be the case whenever grooves, pits or other damage is evident in the bearing surfaces.
7. Buy any replacement parts or an entirely new headset. Make sure you get the right size by taking the old fork and at least one screwed-on headset part to the shop with you to match the new parts for size.

*Installation procedure:*
1. If applicable, get the fixed bearing cups and the fork race installed at the bike shop.
2. Fill both bearing cups with grease, turn the frame upside down and place the bearing retainer (or loose bearing balls) inside the lower fixed bearing cup. If held in a retainer, make sure it is installed so that the balls protrude towards you on the inside where they contact the fork race.
3. Place the fork's steerer tube through the head tube until the fork race seats on the bearing balls in the cup. Hold fork and frame together firmly at this point, then turn it back the right way round.
4. Still holding fork and frame together, place the ball retainer or the loose balls in the upper fixed cup.
5. While continuing to hold fork and frame at the lower headset, screw the adjusting cup on the fork.

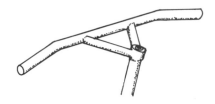

Fig. 16.9 Fixed-stem handlebars

6. Place the lock washer over the adjustable race, with the flat section of the hole matching the corresponding flat section around the circumference of the head tube.
7. Screw the locknut on by hand.
8. Adjust and tighten the bearing as described above.

*Note:*
If the adjusting cup cannot be screwed on far enough to adjust the bearing properly, the threaded portion of the steerer tube is too short. If the locknut can not be tightened down fully, the steerer tube is too long. Let a bike shop mechanic shorten the tube or cut the thread further, as appropriate.

## Handlebars and Stem

Next to the tires, the handlebars most characterize the mountain bike: wide and flat. However, not as wide and not as flat as in the early days of mountain biking. Meanwhile, most of us, manufacturers included, have learned that a width of 55 cm (26 in) is generally more than enough. If the bars are too wide, feel free to use a hacksaw to reduce its width equally on both sides, providing the shape of the bars is such that they can be held and the brakes can be reached comfortably after this kind of surgery. This is important since the bars nowadays are often less straight and flat than they were in the pioneering days.

On a mountain bike of any quality, the handlebars should be adjustable, except perhaps if they are tailored to the particular rider. Adjustability is achieved by means of a separate stem clamped around the bars with a binder bolt. This detail is shown in Fig. 16.8. On fixed designs, shown in Fig. 16.9, the bars are welded to the stem. Both the handlebars and the stem may be of aluminum or steel alloy. The latter is often actually lighter, if a strong enough alloy with a small enough wall thickness and a large enough diameter is selected. Both

Modern mountain bike front end: stem with adjustable bars and a roller guide for the front brake cable.

aluminum and thin-walled steel bars require a reinforcing sleeve that projects at least one inch on either side of the stem's binder clamp.

Though some mountain bike handlebar stems are still of a V-shape pattern, holding the bars at two points, most manufacturers now supply bars with a single stem clamp. The latter should be a little wider and stronger than is the case on a regular bike. Though the V-shape stem attachment is very strong, the problem is that, with today's shorter frame designs, it gets in the way of your knees when standing on the pedals to climb. Most stems have an integral guide and anchor for the front brake cable; on some models the guide takes the form of a roller, which assures minimum cable friction.

The stem itself is held in the fork's steerer tube by means of a wedge or cone shaped item that is pulled into or against the end of the stem by means of an expander bolt. The latter is accessible from the top of the stem. In Chapter 5 you have been shown how to adjust the bars with the aid of this device. Here you will be shown how to replace the stem or the handlebars, which will also be necessary to overhaul the headset or to replace the fork.

### Remove and Install Handlebars with Stem

For this job you need an Allan key to match the expander bolt (usually 6 mm), and sometimes a mallet or a hammer. Before you start, release the front brake tension, as explained in Chapter 21.

*Removal procedure:*
1. Holding the front wheel firmly clamped between your legs, loosen the expander bolt about 4 turns.
2. If the stem comes loose immediately, just pull the combination

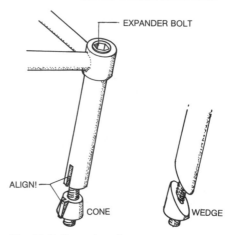

Fig. 16.10 Stem clamping

of stem and bars out.
3. If it does not come loose immediately, raise the wheel off the ground by pulling up from the handlebars; firmly tap on the expander bolt to loosen the wedge or the cone, shown in Fig. 16.10, after which the stem should be loose in the steerer tube. If not, put some thin flowing lubricant in at the point where the stem disappears inside the upper headset locknut and try again after waiting a few minutes. Pull the combination of bar and stem out of the top.

*Installation procedure:*
1. Make sure the expander bolt is loose enough to fit in line with the stem, yet not so loose that the wedge can be turned more than part of a turn. If a conical expander is used instead of a wedge, the ribs on the outside of the cone should lie inside the slots in the stem.
2. Straddle the front wheel, clamping the front wheel between your legs. Insert the stem in the steerer tube at the upper headset. Lower it as far as seems comfortable, making sure at least 6.5 cm (2.5 in) of the stem is seated inside the steerer tube,

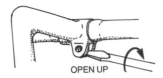

OPEN UP

Fig. 16.11 Releasing handlebars from stem

which is the minimum safe insertion depth.

3. Holding the handlebars straight and at the desired height, tighten the expander bolt firmly.

### Replace Bars or Stem Separately

To sever the connection between stem and handlebars, or to install the one on the other, keep the stem on the bike, so you can use the latter for leverage. You need an Allan key to fit the binder bolt and usually a big screwdriver. Before you proceed to the actual work, release the brakes, as described in Chapter 21; then remove the hand grip, the brake handle and the thumb shifter on at least one side of the bars.

*Removal Procedure:*

1. Holding the bike from the front, clamping the front wheel between your legs, undo the binder bolt or bolts on the stem that hold the handlebars by four or five turns.

2. See whether you can twist the bar out from the stem. Usually the stem fits around the bar too tightly. In that case, use the big screwdriver to wedge open the stem's binder clamp, as shown in Fig. 16.11, perhaps after removing the binder bolt or bolts altogether. Meanwhile, twist the bar while pushing it out of the stem until it can be removed.

*Installation procedure*

1. Remove any accessories that may be installed, at least from one end of the handlebars. Hold the bike from the front, clamping the front wheel between your legs. If you are installing a new item, ascertain that bar and stem match with respect to bar diameter.

2. Open up the stem's binder clamp, while guiding the bar through. When it is centered, tighten the binder bolt somewhat.

3. Move to the rider's position and put the bar in the desired orientation, then tighten the binder bolt fully.

4. Install the various accessories on the bars.

### Different Handlebars

Though most mountain bike riders love the flat bars that make it so easy to reach the brake levers, some more

Bridgestone's drop handlebars with matching stem specifically designed for trail riding. The aluminum alloy bars are flared out to provide wrist clearance and the stem is angled to raise the bar without throwing it forward too much. Bar-end shifters are the obvious choice for this kind of bars.

experienced cyclists prefer drop 'racing' bars, even on their off-road machine. At least one major manufacturer, Bridgestone, actually supplies its top model equipped with a spread out version of drop bars. To get at least more leverage, which is desirable off-road, you may spread the ends of regular drop bars to about 50 cm (20 in, using the technique shown in Fig. 16.12. Again, bars and stem must match with respect to diameter.

### Handgrips

Rigid or foam plastic handgrips are typically used on mountain bikes. The most comfortable are models made of a relatively firm type of foam. To remove or replace them, you may have to add a drop of dishwashing liquid between grip and bar, lifting the grip locally with a screwdriver. To avoid loosening the grips unintentionally, remove all traces of the liquid before installing the handgrips. If you use drop

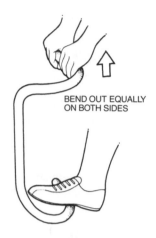

BEND OUT EQUALLY
ON BOTH SIDES

Fig. 16.12 Bending out drop bars

bars, you should probably install foam sleeves, such as Grab-On, rather than conventional handlebar tape, to minimize the numbing effect on the hands caused by vibrations when riding over rough surfaces.

# Saddle and Seatpost

The saddle, or seat, is shown together with the seat post, which connects it to the frame, in Fig. 17.1. On the mountain bike, you will probably spend more time actually sitting on the saddle than you would on a ten-speed derailleur bike with drop handlebars. This is due to the different weight distribution resulting from the higher handlebars and lower saddle position preferred by most mountain bike riders. In addition, downhill riding requires a rather low saddle position, forcing you to rest much of your weight on it, while the lower gearing encourages you to stay seated even when climbing steep inclines.

### The Saddle
For the reasons listed above, the mountain bike saddle had better be comfortable. In contrast to the one mounted on a racing bike, it serves

This curious machine by German frame builder Sattler sports the most the most comfortable saddle: the double wire, sprung Brooks 66 Champion.

more as a seat and less as a guide. This does not apply for some of the more competitively experienced riders, who prefer to sit on their mountain bikes the way they do on a racing machine. For all others, the mountain bike saddle should be shaped differently. Though still long and narrow at the front, it should be wider and softer, yet resilient near the back, where most of the weight rests. Such saddles, often referred to as anatomic models, are padded versions of nylon saddles, patterned after Italian and French women's models.

These saddles were originally designed for a more inclined posture than is typical on a mountain bike, but are wide enough to accommodate the typically wider pelvic structure of most women. They also suit a man in mountain biking posture. So women may need even wider models if they ride a mountain bike. You can estimate the correct overall saddle width, referring to Fig. 17.2, if you measure the distance A between the bony protrusions

of the pelvis and add at least 4 inches. Use this figure if you are slightly built, more if you are heavier in this part of your physique.

Though padded nylon saddles that are covered with a thin layer of leather and models made entirely of plastic are the trend of the times, I have a different preference. My favorite saddle, illustrated in Fig. 17.3, is the sprung leather Brooks 66 saddle, or its slightly fancier and narrower counterpart the Brooks 66 Champion. Hard to find in the US, but worth asking for (Sturmey Archer, with US headquarters in Chicago, is the supplier). These are self supporting leather saddles with double wires and coil springs in the back. Beautiful items and quite reasonably priced, considering what people pay for the plastic junk typically installed on mountain bikes.

Mounting this double-wire saddle is a little tricky, since the regular seatpost accepts only a single wire on each side. Angell and Breeze of California make a very elegant adaptor plate, shown in Fig. 17.4, which goes between the two springs and mounts on a regular seatpost. Alternately, you can make one yourself, as shown in Fig. 17.5. Virtually all leather saddles are equipped with sturdy eyelets for the attachment of a saddle bag, which I consider very useful. If your saddle does not have them, you may be able to round up a saddle bag mounting clamp.

### The Seat Post

The saddle is attached to the frame by means of a seat post, which in turn is clamped in the frame's seat lug by a binder bolt. On the mountain bike, this binder bolt invariably takes the form of a quick-release. The seatpost, some models of which are depicted in Fig. 17.6, should take the form of an aluminum forging with an adjustor to

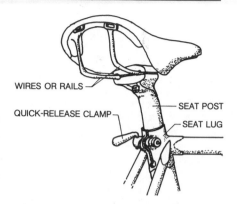

Fig. 17.1 Saddle and seatpost

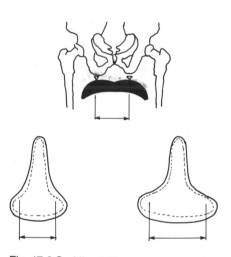

Fig. 17.2 Saddle width

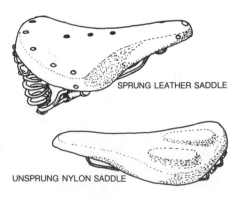

Fig. 17.3 Saddle types

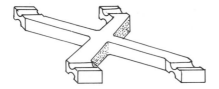

Fig. 17.4 Double-wire adaptor

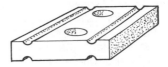

Fig. 17.5 Home-made adaptor

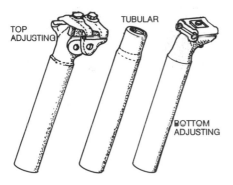

Fig. 17.6 Seat post types

vary the saddle angle relative to the horizontal plane.

Some cheap bikes may have a plain tubular steel seatpost that allows adjustment of the saddle angle only in very big steps. On the other end of the scale are models with a high strength tubular steel alloy section on which an aluminum precision adjusting mechanism is attached. The latter are generally both stronger and lighter than any of the other models. These are particularly useful when the seatpost has to be very long in order to accommodate a high saddle position on a small bike.

The diameter of the tubular section of any seatpost must match the inside diameter of the bike's seat tube. It should slide easily up and down when the binder bolt is loosened, yet hold firmly when it is tightened. The right diameter depends on the bike in question, the most common size for steel mountain bike frames being 26.8 mm.

To assure that the seatpost slides freely up and down to allow height adjustment, make sure the inside of the seat lug and the upper portion of the seat tube are both perfectly smooth. Moving the seat up or down should not leave any scratches on the seatpost. If necessary, treat the inside of the seat tube with a fine file or abrasive paper. The slot in the seat lug and the seat tube that is clamped closed to tighten the saddle should be quite long, at least 2 mm (³⁄₃₂ in) wide, and end in a round hole, at least 4 mm (³⁄₁₆ in) in diameter. This prevents the formation of cracks at the end of the slot, resulting from frequent use of the quick-release binder bolt.

For mountain bike use, the seatpost should be at least 300 mm long to assure adequate up-and-down adjustability. At least 65 mm (2½ in) of this must remain inside the seat tube even

Fine, so-called 'fastback' seat cluster detail on Mountain Goat bike by Jeff Lindsay.

when the saddle is in its highest position, so that it is held adequately. If the manufacturer has not provided a corresponding mark that shows how much may protrude, you may mark it yourself, using either a scratching pin or an indelible marker.

### Quick-Release Binder Bolt

To use the quick-release binder bolt, shown in Fig. 17.7, realize that it should not be tightened by screwing or unscrewing, but by flipping the lever. On many high quality bikes, similar quick-release mechanisms are also installed in the wheel hubs to allow fast and convenient removal and installation of the wheels. As a saddle adjusting device, quick-releases are essentially used only on mountain bikes.

The thumb nut at one end must be screwed on just so far that the mechanism is just loose enough in the untensioned position of the lever. Then a flick of the quick-release lever should tighten it enough to hold it firmly. If it can't be pushed over all the way, loosen it first and then unscrew the thumb nut perhaps half a turn, after which try again. Conversely,

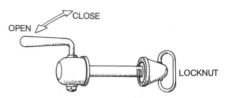

Fig. 17.7 Quick-release binder bolt

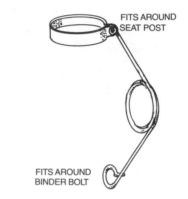

Fig. 17.8 Hite-Rite

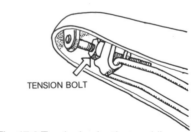

Fig. 17.9 Tensioning leather saddle

SunTour quick-release binder bolt assembly.

tighten the nut a little in the open position if it is too loose with the lever closed.

### Hite-Rite

Many top-line mountain bikes are equipped with an ingenious spring mechanism called Hite Rite, shown in Fig. 17.8 and produced by mountain bike pioneers Breeze and Angell. This device has a spring which is held around the binder bolt at the lower end and has a clip that is clamped and bolted around the seatpost on the

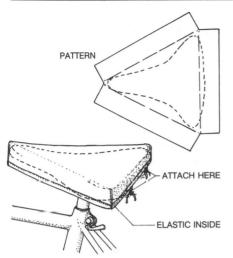

PATTERN

ATTACH HERE

ELASTIC INSIDE

Fig. 17.10 Saddle cover

way to apply it is from underneath. Repeat the treatment at least twice a year, or whenever it has dried after getting wet.

If you have a leather saddle and it does get wet, do not sit on it until it is completely dry, to prevent permanent deformation of the stiff leather cover. Even if you don't purposely leave the bike out in the rain, a soaking may occur accidentally while transporting the bike on top of a car or in a pick-up.

Long's the word on mountain bike seat posts. This is SunTour's SP 2000, measuring a full 330 mm. If that's not enough, you need a bigger frame.

upper end. Even if your bike was not supplied with one, I recommend buying this accessory, since it makes adjusting a lot easier and more accurate. This handy gadget also protects your saddle against theft.

This mechanism allows the saddle to be adjusted while riding – down with some of your weight on it, and up while standing on the pedals. Perhaps the greatest benefit is the fact that it guides the saddle perfectly parallel to its original orientation. To install the Hite-Rite, first attach it loosely around the seatpost and place the other end around the binder bolt. Then put the saddle in the highest position you will ever want it to be, and tighten the clamp around the seatpost.

**Saddle and Seatpost Maintenance**
The saddle itself needs very little care, unless it is a leather model, such as the ones I recommend. These should be treated with saddle soap, neat's foot oil or Brooks Proofide from time to time to keep the leather supple and to prevent the penetration of water. The least economic, but most effective

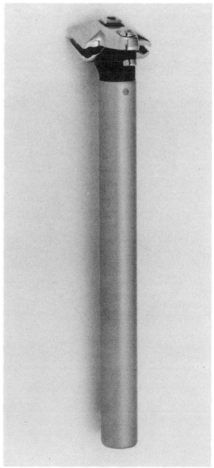

If you have to transport your bike that way, wrap the saddle with a plastic bag to keep it dry if there is even the slightest chance of rain.

From time to time, when a leather saddle cover loses its shape and tension, it should be tightened. To do this, adjust the tensioning bolt shown in Fig. 17.9 by screwing the nut further onto the bolt, pushing the nose of the saddle further out.

Any saddle can be protected against rain and abuse by means of a saddle cover. You may be able to buy one ready made. If you are like me, you'll want to sew your own. Use coated nylon pack cloth and sew it together as shown in Fig. 17.10. You may either keep it on all the time, or you may just put it over the saddle when you leave the bike somewhere, attaching it by means of two straps in the back.

The only other work involving the saddle system is to protect the seat-post, the binder bolt and the Hite-Rite – if installed – against dirt and corrosion. A little vaseline, applied sparingly with a cloth takes care of the corrosion on the seat post, while the other mechanisms are best cleaned with a brush or a rag, after which you may apply a thin spray lubricant, such as WD-40 or the lightest grade of LPS. Finally, remove any excess lubricant with a clean rag.

# 18
# The Drivetrain

The mountain bike's transmission comprises the various components that transmit the rider's effort to the rear wheel: crankset with bottom bracket and chainwheels, pedals, chain and freewheel. The derailleur system, which allows this transmission to operate at the desired gear ratio, will be treated separately in the next chapter. Though each one of the components described here is also installed on other bikes, most of them are designed differently for mountain bike use. This is necessary to stand up to the particular kind of treatment they receive off-road on a mountain bike.

### The Crankset
The crankset can be considered the heart of the drivetrain. It comprises several different components, which will each be described in the following sections. These are the bottom bracket with its bearings, the cranks, and

Typical mountain bike drivetrain. Though these chainwheels are round, everything else is standard on virtually all mountain bikes these days. This chapter introduces the various components.

the chainwheels. Generally, all these components are supplied as a group of matching parts by the same manufacturer. However, it is entirely possible to select parts from various manufacturers or different models to make up the system.

### The Bottom Bracket
Sometimes referred to as crank hanger in Britain, the bottom bracket is the set of bearings that lie in the frame's bottom bracket shell, together with the spindle or axle to which the cranks are attached. For mountain bikes, two types are relatively common: the conventional adjustable BSA bearing illustrated in Fig. 18.1 and the system with cartridge bearings shown in Fig. 18.2. On both types, the spindle usually has tapered square ends for the installation of cotterless cranks.

On hight quality bottom brackets, the spindle is hollow and the cranks are held with bolts, while some cheaper models use solid axles with threaded protrusions to which the cranks are held with nuts. Whatever

type of bearing or spindle is used, the longer end of the axle projecting from the unit goes on the RH or chain side of the bike.

Though the cartridge bearing is often thought to be superior, the size of the bearings relative to the total unit is actually bigger on the adjustable model, which makes that one stronger, all else being equal. Consequently, as long as parts of adequate quality are used and they are adjusted and lubricated regularly, the latter can give excellent service. They are certainly not inherently inferior to the cartridge bearing variety, as is sometimes implied.

If you've never heard of cartridge bearing units, it's because of the almost universal use of the incorrect term *sealed bearing*, when, in fact, cartridge bearing is meant. Either type of bottom bracket can be provided with some kind of seals to keep dirt out and lubricant in. Neither type can be perfectly sealed, so some kind of cleaning and lubrication will be required from time to time. This is easier on the adjustable model than it is on the cartridge type, which may have to be replaced in its entirety.

### Bottom Bracket Maintenance

To take a look at the cartridge bearing units first, little maintenance work is possible. Many times they can actually be cleaned and lubricated (though indeed not adjusted). A little careful manipulation of the seal with a very thin small screwdriver generally allows you to remove it. Rinsing with a thick oil will both clean and lubricate the unit. Disadvantage: you have to keep repeating this process frequently once you start it, since the oil will run out again. Unsealed units can be lubricated the same way, which should be done after every long ride in dusty or wet terrain.

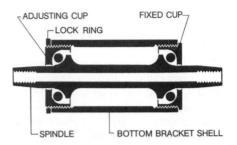

Fig. 18.1 Adjustable bearing bottom bracket

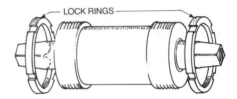

Fig. 18.2 Cartridge bearing bottom bracket

The only other maintenance operations you can easily carry out yourself on the cartridge bearing bottom bracket are side-to-side adjustment and replacement. The former may be necessary to adjust the chain line: to align the plane of the middle chainring with that of the middle sprocket (or, on a freewheel with six sprockets, with the middle of the freewheel block). On many designs these units are held in the bottom bracket shell by means of an internal spring clip. In this case the side-by-side adjustment is only possible on certain models, such as the one used on Fisher MountainBikes. Other units are equipped with an adjustment ring on the LH side, allowing this adjustment by loosening the lockring. Subsequently, the whole unit can be moved either to the left or the right, using the special matching bottom bracket tools, and then tightened in the new position.

The conventional way to lubricate any kind of bicycle bearing is with grease, which is packed inside the

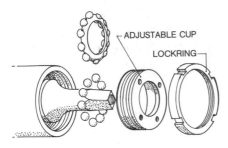

ADJUSTABLE CUP

LOCKRING

Fig. 18.3 Bottom bracket adjustment

bearing races where the bearing balls are embedded. This is done in the factory and must be repeated at least once a season for all adjustable units. To do this, first lift the chain off the chainwheel and remove the cranks, as described in the appropriate sections below. Now proceed as follows, using either improvised tools or, preferably, the special wrenches for the particular make and model installed on your bike. These are available from most bike shops. Proceed as follows:

1. Remove the lockring on the LH side by unscrewing it to the left (see Fig. 18.3).
2. Remove the bearing cup on the LH side by unscrewing it to the left, while catching the bearing balls, which may lie loose or may be held in a retainer, when it comes off.
3. Pull the spindle out, catching the bearing balls, on the other side.
4. Clean all parts and inspect them. Replace anything that is pitted, grooved, damaged or corroded.
5. Generally, the fixed bearing cup can be left in place on the LH side. If it must be replaced, remember that it has LH thread (at least on most bikes sold in the US and Britain). Consequently, it must be removed by turning to the right, and installed by turning to the left.
6. Pack the cups with bearing grease, then reassemble in reverse order and adjust, following the procedure below.

*Note:*
Though special tools are preferable, improvised tools may be used for this and many other jobs – very carefully. To loosen or tighten the lockring, use a blunt screwdriver and a hammer, tapping the lockring from the notches in the circumference. To loosen or tighten the adjustable bearing race, use a hammer and a drift or similar roughly pointed object with a blunt end. To remove or tighten the fixed or RH cup, use either a really big adjustable wrench (crescent wrench), or clamp the cup in a metalworking vice with the frame horizontal, and turn the latter. To assure correct alignment, always finish the removal and start the installation process by hand, rather than using tools, whether provisional or not.

## Adjust Bottom Bracket

After overhauling the bottom bracket, or anytime the adjustable bearing is loose, it must be adjusted. Cartridge bearings are not adjustable and must be replaced. This job should be left to a bike shop, unless you have the special tools and appropriate skills to do it yourself. To adjust a BSA bottom bracket, you need the same tools as for overhauling.

1. Loosen the lockring by one turn, unscrewing to the left.
2. Loosen or tighten the adjustable bearing cup as appropriate.
3. Retighten the lockring, making sure the adjustable cup does not turn with it, restraining it with the matching tool.
4. If necessary, repeat the procedure until the bearing runs smoothly without play. Smoothness of operation is checked by hand, preferably with the cranks removed; looseness of the bearings is best established using the leverage of the installed crank.

## The Cranks

Virtually all mountain bikes have aluminum cranks that are attached to the ends of the bottom bracket spindle by means of a cotterless device, depicted in Fig. 18.4. In this system the crank has a square tapered hole that matches the square tapered end of the spindle. A bolt – or sometimes a nut, if the bottom bracket spindle is not hollow but has threaded projections – clamps the crank over the spindle and a dustcap covers the recess from the outside.

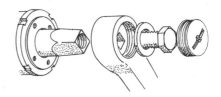

Fig. 18.4 Cotterless crank attachment

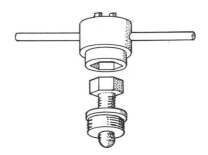

Fig. 18.5 Crank tool

The RH crank is equipped with an attachment spider for the chainwheels. The pattern of the holes in the latter varies greatly from make to make and even from model to model. It must correspond to the particular chainwheels installed. On a new bike the manufacturer installs cranks and chainwheels from the same manufacturer. In fact, a complete standard crankset, including cranks, as well as bottom bracket and chainwheels from the same component manufacturer, is generally installed. When replacing either cranks or chainwheels, the interchangeability restrictions must be considered.

The square taper is not standardized. Thus, you may find when replacing either the cranks or the bottom bracket, that a crank either hits the chainstay or conversely does not seat fully on the spindle. Consult a bike shop to find out what fits and what doesn't. A comprehensive source of interchangeability information in general is *Sutherland's Handbook for Bicycle Mechanics*, which any good bike shop should have available for reference.

Cranks are made in several different lengths. Some mountain bike riders swear by longer cranks, rather than the standard length of 170 mm. This dimension is measured from the center of the bottom bracket spindle

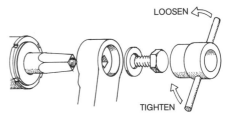

Fig. 18.6 Tighten or loosen crank attachment bolt

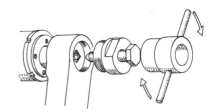

Fig. 18.7 Extract crank

hole to the center of the pedal hole. If you have longer legs than average, a longer crank of 175 or 180 mm may be justified.

## Crank Maintenance

We'll cover two maintenance jobs here: tightening, and replacement. The crank attachment must be tightened when the square tapered hole is not fully seated on the spindle's square end. The crank has to be replaced when the crank cracks or gets bent and no amount of straightening will do the trick. You can tell when a crank is bent, since the pedal develops a straight wobbling behavior, usually after a fall. Leave the straightening to a bike shop, since it requires a special tool. The simple tool depicted in Fig. 18.5 for removing and tightening the crank, on the other hand, is something you should buy yourself. Make sure it fits the particular crankset installed on your bike.

## Tighten Crank

To do this, you need a crank extractor tool matching the particular make and model of crankset installed on your bike. Actually, you only need the wrench part of this two-part tool, but you have to buy the whole thing, which should be done when you buy the bike, so you have it on hand when needed. You will most need it within the first few weeks, when the material of the crank is deforming slightly. Refer to Fig. 18.5 and Fig. 18.6 for this job.

1. Remove the dustcap, using a fitting tool or a coin, depending on its shape.
2. Tighten the bolt or the nut that lies under the dust cap, using the wrench part of the crank tool.
3. Reinstall the dust cap.

## Replace Cranks

This operation may be necessary in order to do bottom bracket maintenance or to replace a defective crank or bottom bracket part. For this work, you need both parts of the crank ex-

tractor tool to match the particular make and model of your crankset. Refer to Fig. 18.5 and Fig. 18.7.

*Removal procedure:*
1. Remove the dustcap, using a fitting tool or coin.
2. Restraining the crank, unscrew the bolt or the nut that lies under the dustcap. Remove both the bolt or the nut *and the underlying washer*.
3. Withdraw the inner part of the extractor part of the crank tool and thread it into the threaded recess in the crank as far as it will go.
4. Restraining the outer part of the tool that is installed in the crank, screw in the inner part, which pulls the crank off the spindle.
5. Restraining the crank, unscrew the tool from the crank.

*Installation procedure:*
1. Inspect all contact surfaces and all parts, to make sure they are clean and free from serious corrosion or damage. Sparingly apply lubricant to the threaded parts, as well as the matching surfaces of spindle and crank hole.
2. Place the cranks on the spindle, 180° offset from each other, making sure the one with the chainwheel attachment spider is on the RH side.
3. Install the washer, followed by the bolt or the nut; then tighten the latter with the wrench part of the crank tool, restraining the crank.
4. Install the dustcap.
5. At about 50 mile intervals during the first 200 miles, retighten the bolt until it is fully seated.

## The Chainwheels

These items, also referred to as chainrings, are available in a wide range of sizes for the mountain bike. Generally, three are installed, as described in the chapters devoted to the gearing system. In this chapter, we shall ignore gearing theory and size selection, looking only at the mechanical aspects of the chainwheels.

They are attached to the RH crank by one of the methods shown in Fig. 18.8. In my experience, the method shown in the RH detail is generally the more satisfactory. It results in greater strength and rigidity, leading to fewer cases of bent and buckled chainwheels. Of course, it also depends on the hardness of the materials used, which accounts for a lot of the price difference between superficially similar cranksets.

Most mountain bikes, particularly those intended for less experienced riders, are equipped with chainwheels that are not truly round. Shimano's Biopace and SR's Ovaltech designs are the most popular of these. Though more expensive, they are used almost universally on quality mountain bikes as an incentive to the novice cyclist. Curiously enough, accomplished riders almost invariably prefer round chainwheels.

The only justification for the odd off-round designs is found in the inefficient low pedalling speeds novice riders use. This results in an irregular force distribution over the pedal cycle. True, the odd-shaped chainwheels are one way to solve the problem. But only temporarily. The preferable solution is to practice cycling at a higher pedalling rate, changing down to the appropriate gear to do so.

### Chainwheel Maintenance

The maintenance operations that may be required comprise straightening a chainwheel when either the teeth or the entire unit is bent, as well as disassembly or removal to replace one that is worn or damaged. Fig. 18.9 will help you identify a worn chainwheel.

If only individual teeth are bent, you can grab each of these separately with a crescent wrench that is ad-

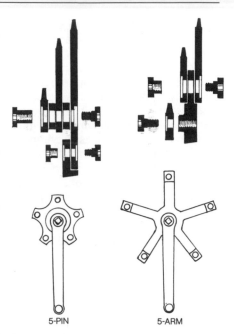

5-PIN                    5-ARM

Fig. 18.8 Chainwheel attachment

NEW                    WORN

Fig. 18.9 The signs of wear on a chainwheel

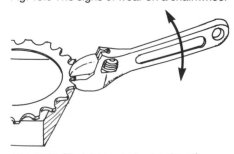

Fig. 18.10 Straighten chainwheel teeth

justed to just fit. Then bend it back carefully, as illustrated in Fig. 18.10. Inspect the result, replacing any chainwheel on which teeth are either seriously damaged, cracked or broken.

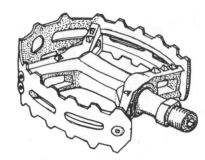

Fig. 18.11 Bear claw pedal

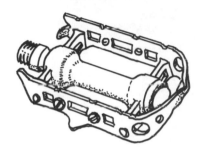

Fig. 18.12 Regular quill pedal

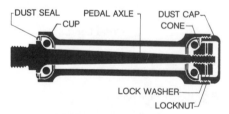

Fig. 18.13 Pedal cross section

If the entire chainwheel is warped, resulting in intermittent scraping of the chain against the cage of the front derailleur or the RH chainstay, you can use a wedge-shaped piece of wood to carefully straighten it out. A crude roadside alternative may be to use a wide screwdriver instead. If you have particularly soft chainwheels, such as some of the cheapest models and the now rarely used ones made by the French TA company, you may use a mallet to straighten the entire chainwheel. If in doubt, I suggest you take it to a bike shop or replace the entire chainwheel.

To replace the chainwheels, simply loosen the bolts that hold the chainwheels to the spider or to each other, countering at the other side. Take care not to lose any of the bolts, nuts and washers, also noting where each of these parts was installed. In the case of the Shimano Biopace and other non-round chainwheels, observe where the label sits relative to the RH, crank and reinstall it with the label in the same place.

### The Pedals

Mountain bike pedals are designed for more grip on regular shoes than those installed on ten-speed bikes. In addition to the awe-inspiring bear claw models, shown in Fig. 18.11, there are slightly narrower metal ones, while some cheap bikes have pedals made of moulded resin embedded graphite fiber. My preference is for those that most closely resemble the conventional quill pedals, as illustrated in Fig. 18.12.

At least as important as the pedal's exterior shape are its guts, shown in Fig. 18.13 for a typical mountain bike pedal. The most important difference relative to any old pedal is that there should be a dust seal on the crank side bearing. Some models have cartridge bearings, which are not necessarily superior. Though they are better sealed and probably run perfectly smoothly when new, the cartridge bearings must be replaced in their entirety when they develop play or run rough.

### Remove and Install Pedal

This job has to be carried out whenever either the cranks or the pedals are replaced, or in order to store or transport the bike. All you need is a wrench that fits the stub with which the pedal is screwed into the crank. It is best done with the crank installed on the bike, proceeding as follows:

*Removal procedure:*
1. Restrain the crank, if necessary with a rod stuck through the frame. To remove the RH pedal, stop the crank from turning counterclockwise, clockwise to remove the LH pedal.
2. Using a thin, flat wrench, grab the flattened section of the stub that is screwed into the crank. If the stub has a hexagonal recess, use an Allen key from the back of the crank to remove the pedal. Unscrew the RH pedal to the left, the LH pedal, which has LH screw thread, to the right.

*Installation procedure:*
1. Inspect all threaded parts to make sure they are clean and undamaged, then put a little lubricant on them. To protect the crank face, you may install a thin steel washer that fits around the threaded stub on the pedal axle, also applying a little grease there.
2. Establish which is the RH pedal and which the LH one, consulting Fig. 18.14 if they are not appropriately marked.
3. Carefully aligning the threads, screw the pedal in as far as you can by hand. Holding the crank in place with one hand, screw the RH pedal in clockwise, the LH pedal counterclockwise.
4. Restraining the crank as appropriate, tighten the pedal with the wrench.

**Pedal Maintenance**
The bearings may have to be lubricated or adjusted when the pedal bearings are loose or do not run smoothly. If the problem cannot be eliminated this way, replace the entire pedal or just the latter if the problem is

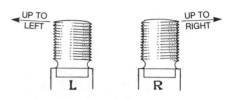

Fig. 18.14 RH and LH pedal thread

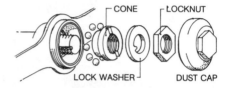

Fig. 18.15 Pedal adjusting parts

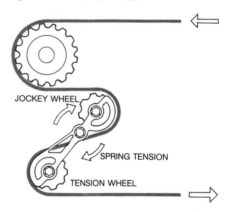

Fig. 18.16 Chain routing

due to a bent axle, following the instructions below for assembly and disassembly. You will need a wrench or prizing tool to remove the dustcap, a wrench to fit the locknut underneath, either a wrench or a thin screwdriver to adjust the bearing cone, and sometimes a small screwdriver or Allan wrench to remove the cage of the pedal if it hinders access to the bearing. Refer to Fig. 18.15 for this work.

1. Remove the dustcap.
2. Remove the locknut, or merely loosen it 2–3 turns if you only want to adjust the bearing, without lubrication or part replacement.

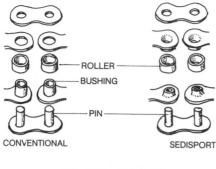

CONVENTIONAL          SEDISPORT

Fig. 18.17 Chain construction

3. Lift up the keyed lock washer and tighten or loosen the underlying bearing cone as appropriate to adjust the bearing. Remove these parts to overhaul or lubricate the pedal.
4. To overhaul or lubricate, pull the pedal housing off, catching the bearing balls on both ends. Replace or clean and lubricate all the parts, packing the bearing cups with grease, after which the bearing balls are embedded in the grease.
5. Reinstall in reverse order, then adjust as explained under point 3 above.
6. Tighten the locknut, restraining the adjustable bearing cone, e.g. with the thin screwdriver. If the cone can't be stopped from turning, replace the lock washer, making sure the key that fits in the groove of the pedal axle is not worn off so far that the washer can turn on the axle.
7. When the pedal operates smoothly, reinstall the dustcap and, if appropriate, the pedal cage.

### The Chain

Mountain bikes are equipped with the same ½ x ³⁄₃₂ in chains that are used on other derailleur bikes. These dimensions refer to the length between two consecutive pins and the internal width between the inner link plates, respectively. The chain should be long enough to wrap around the largest chainwheel, the largest sprocket and the derailleur pulleys as shown in Fig. 18.16, while still leaving a little spring travel in the derailleur mechanism.

Two typical chain constructions are shown in Fig. 18.17. If the bike has a freewheel block with 6 or 7 sprockets, you should use a narrow chains. These have the same nominal dimensions and the same internal size, but the pins protrude less far. Personally, I don't like the kind of chain with 'bulging' link plates, because they wear and literally stretch. Just the same, the latter are extremely popular on account of their greater lateral flexibility which eases shifting. All the hot US riders use the Shimano Dura Ace narrow chain which is of that design, while virtually all Europeans prefer the Sedisport chain, which lasts much longer.

Bash plate to protect the drive-train on Range Rider bicycle from Cleland in England.

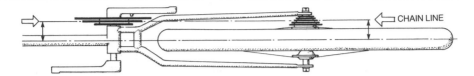

Fig. 18.18 Chain line

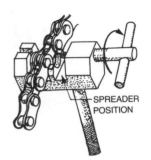

Fig. 18.19 Chain tool use

## Chain Line
The chain line, illustrated in Fig. 18.18, should preferably be such that the intermediate chainwheel lines up perfectly with the middle sprocket on a freewheel block with five or seven sprockets, or the point between the third and the fourth if it has 6 sprockets. Unfortunately, this situation is very hard to achieve with a mountain bike, due to the constraints of the bike's geometry. Since the correct chain line results in less lateral twisting of the chain and guarantees the most efficient transmission of power, as well as the smoothest gear shifting possible, you should at least try to optimize it. Corrections to the chain line are made by adjusting the bottom bracket, by inserting spacers, or by straightening the frame if it is bent. These jobs are best left to an experienced bike shop mechanic.

## Chain Maintenance
The chain is removed, installed, lengthened or shortened by means of the chain tool illustrated in Fig. 18.19. Frequent cleaning and lubrication of the chain contributes to drivetrain efficiency. Though it is possible to lubricate the chain on the bike, the most thorough way is to remove it. Rinse it in a solvent, such as kerosene (paraffin in Britain), mixed with about one part in ten of mineral oil, which prevents rust and provides lubrication in hidden nooks and crannies. Let it drip dry and then immediately lubricate it with a waxy lubricant, such as special motorcycle chain lube. Wipe the exterior off with a rag. This lubrication will last about six weeks in rainy weather on the road, twice as long in dry weather – but still only one day under dusty off-road conditions.

If you never take the bike out in wet weather, especially if dust is your primary problem, you may consider lubricating the chain in paraffin (American paraffin this time, which is known as candle wax in Britain). Don't heat it directly on the hot plate, but in a can that's standing in a saucepan with boiling water. When the paraffin is liquid, take the can out of the boiling water and dip the chain in. Let it soak about one minute, then remove it before the paraffin begins to solidify. Wipe the exterior of the chain with a rag while it's still hot.

## Chain Removal and Installation
The chain has to be removed to allow thorough lubrication or to be replaced. It wears with use and must be replaced by a new one from time to time – I'd say once a year. Follow these same instructions to shorten or lengthen the chain.

If the chain seems to jump off the largest sprocket after it has been replaced, it may be due either to a stiff link or a worn sprocket. First check for a stiff link, which can be loosened as explained under point 6 of *Installation procedure* below. If that does not do the trick, replace the sprocket or the entire freewheel assembly, since this means the sprocket has been worn down by the old chain. To remove or install the chain, all you need is a chain rivet tool and a rag, proceeding as follows:

*Removal procedure:*
1. Place the tool on one of the pins somewhere midway between chainwheel and sprockets, as shown in Fig. 18.19. Turn the handle until the pin of the tool pushes against the pin of the chain.
2. Turn the handle clockwise by 6 full turns, which pushes the pin out of the chain far enough without allowing it to come unseated.

SunTour competition pedals, suitable for the installation of toeclips.

3. Screw the handle back, so you can retract the tool.
4. Wriggle the chain apart. If it can't be done yet, reinstall the tool and give it another half turn or so and try again.

*Note:*
If you should push the pin out all the way, install some new links, which you can pick up at a bike shop, making sure they are of the same chain make and model. Remove a section of your old chain and insert this part instead.

*Installation procedure:*
1. To establish the correct length, wrap the chain around the largest chainwheel, the largest sprocket and both derailleur pulleys (referring to Fig. 18.16), passing through the front derailleur cage. Determine its correct length so there is a little spring movement left in the derailleur mechanism, lengthening or shortening the chain as appropriate.

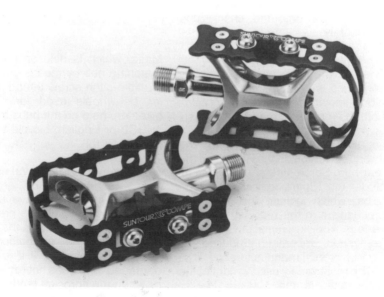

2. Place the chain on a combination of the smallest chainwheel and an intermediate or small sprocket, to release the spring tension in the derailleur, still keeping it routed as before.
3. Place the inside of the protruding pin in the hole of the corresponding link at the other end of the chain and hold the two ends together.
4. Place the chain rivet tool over the pin and screw the handle in, making sure the pin is pushed through the bushing and comes out the other end. If not, wriggle the various parts relative to each other until they line up.
5. Retract the tool when the pin protrudes equally far as the other pins on both sides.
6. Check whether the links are flexible with respect to each other at this point. If not, twist the chain sideways until they are freed. Alternatively, place the chain in the other position of the chain tool (the one marked spreader slot in Fig. 18.19) and gently turn in the handle about a quarter of a turn to loosen the links. If necessary, repeat from the other side until the chain runs smoothly.

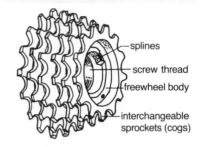

Fig. 18.20 Freewheel block

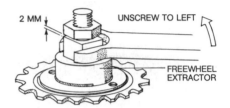

Fig. 18.21 Freewheel tool use

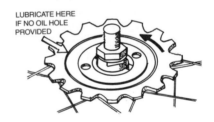

Fig. 18.22 Freewheel lubrication

### The Freewheel

The freewheel mechanism is usually contained in a separate freewheel block, shown in Fig. 18.20. It contains both the mechanism and the five, six or seven sprockets. Generally, it is a separate unit screwed onto the threaded portion on the RH side of the rear hub. Some different solutions include the Shimano cassette type hubs, which include the freewheel mechanism in the rear hub, and the various quick replacement type freewheels recently introduced by various French manufacturers.

The most widely used variant of the latter type is the Maillard Helico-Matic, which is held on the special matching hub by means of a special multiple-pitch screw thread. All regular freewheels used for mountain bikes are held on the hubs by means of BCI, or English, bicycle threading (1.370 x 24 tpi).

### Freewheel Removal and Installation

The freewheel may have to be removed and reinstalled in order to replace a broken spoke on the RH side of the rear wheel. In addition, it may have to be replaced if it is worn or damaged and does not run smoothly, or when the sprocket teeth are worn, so the chain jumps or skips teeth. You will need a large crescent wrench and a special freewheel tool to match the make and model of the freewheel used on your bike. Special freewheel mechanisms, such as the Shimano cassette system are best left to a bike shop for maintenance. Proceed as follows:

1. Remove the rear wheel from the bike (see Chapter 20) and place it in front of you with the freewheel side facing up, after removing the axle nuts or the quick-release.
2. Place the freewheel tool over the splines or notches of your freewheel, then reinstall the axle nut or quick-release with about 2 mm ($^3$⁄$_{32}$ in), as shown in Fig. 18.21.
3. Restraining the wheel, e.g. by stemming it with your body against two perpendicular walls in the corner of a room, use the crescent wrench to turn the freewheel tool to the left.
4. After one or two turns, when the freewheel tool hits the axle nut or the quick-release, loosen the nut by another two turns.
5. Repeat steps 3 and 4 until the freewheel comes off easily by hand.

*Installation procedure:*
1. Inspect all screw threaded surfaces for damage, wear and corrosion. Clean or replace parts as appropriate and lubricate the threaded surfaces using grease or vaseline sparingly.
2. Place the wheel horizontally in front of you with the threaded side of the hub facing up.
3. Carefully align the thread on the freewheel with that of the hub, then screw it on by hand as far as it will go.
4. Final tightening of the freewheel takes place 'automatically' when you have installed the wheel on the bike and you apply force to the pedals.

**Freewheel Lubrication**

I do not suggest carrying out any involved overhauling or adjusting work on the freewheel. However, it makes sense to lubricate it when it shows signs of imperfect running. If symptoms persist, either take it to a bike shop, replace it by a new one, or consult my *Bicycle Repair Book* to overhaul the guts of your freewheel.

To lubricate the freewheel mechanism, place the bike on its side with the freewheel facing up and with a shallow can under the other side of

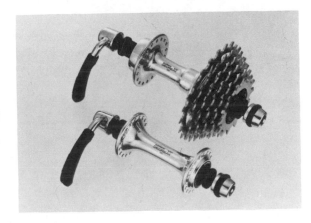

Shimano Deore XT hub set with quick-releases. The one in the rear is a cassette freehub: it has a built-in freewheel mechanism, while the block of six sprockets is held on in splines.

the hub to catch excess lubricant. Using a oil can with a thin spout, pour SAE 30 or thicker oil into the gap between the moving and stationary part of the mechanism, as shown in Fig. 18.22, turning the freewheel in the freewheeling mode. If it has a special oil nipple, such as is standard on the SunTour Winner freewheel, enter the oil through it. Either way, keep pouring in oil until what comes out the other side is about as clean as what you pour in. Let it drip, catching the excess, and wipe everything clean when finished. Take the recovered oil to a gas station for disposal.

# Derailleur Mechanisms

The theoretical aspects of the mountain bike's derailleur gearing system were discussed fully in Chapter 6, while the mechanical details of sprockets and chainwheels were covered in Chapter 18. Here we shall concentrate on the derailleur mechanisms and their control devices: thumb shifters and cables. Refer to Fig. 19.1 for the nomenclature of the various major components of your derailleur system.

On the mountain bike, special versions of derailleurs and shifters are used. The derailleurs accommodate the wide range gearing typically used on these bikes, while the shifters are designed to be installed on top of the handlebars. Indexed rear derailleurs have taken over on mountain bikes completely in the last few years. These replace conventional derailleur systems, on which there are no definite positions of the shift lever for the individual gears selected.

**The Rear Derailleur**

Fig. 19.2 illustrates a typical indexed mountain bike rear derailleur. It comprises a spring-tensioned hinged parallelogram mechanism that is free to pivot over a certain arc around the mounting bolt, and to which a spring-tensioned cage with two little wheels or pulleys is attached at the other end. Inside the mechanism is a ratchet device that has steps corresponding to the lateral cage travel necessary to engage each of the sprocket positions that correspond to the various gears.

When the cable is pulled or released, the mechanism moves over to the next position to the left or the right, corresponding to a different gear. As your pedalling motion pulls the chain forward, it is guided by the two pulleys in the cage to the next sprocket position, engaging the appropriate higher or lower gear. The amount of cable travel is determined by means of the shift lever, which in turn also has a

Shimano indexed rear derailleur and a set of thumb shifters. The bottom one is intended for use with the rear derailleur. If problems develop in the indexed mode, the regular friction mode can be selected with a small auxiliary lever.

ratchet mechanism, stepped to correspond to these same rear derailleur positions.

Even today, not all derailleurs are of the indexed type. There are lots of people who bought their equipment a few years ago, before the advent of the SIS and Accushift craze, and feel no desire to replace their derailleur system just yet. In fact, some of us more experienced riders still prefer the old fashioned derailleurs. We only had to develop a little more sensitivity to master the art of shifting. Indeed, some top-line mountain bikes continue to be supplied with regular derailleurs. This equipment is quite similar, except that there are no ratchet mechanisms in the rear derailleur and its shifter.

The wide gearing range of mountain bike derailleurs is achieved with a very long cage, with the two pulleys lying quite far apart. Virtually all wide-range derailleurs available in the US are those made by either Shimano or SunTour. European manufacturers offering similar products include Sachs-Huret, Simplex and Campagnolo. Though they work as well as their oriental counterparts, they are rarely used in the US.

### Rear Derailleur Maintenance
The most frequent maintenance job on the rear derailleur is the adjustment of the lateral travel for the cage.

Fig. 19.1 The derailleur system

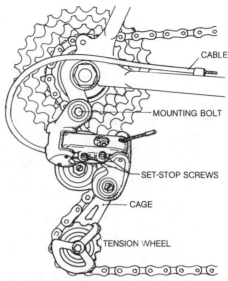

Fig. 19.2 Rear derailleur

This adjustment is needed whenever the chain gets shifted past the biggest or smallest sprocket, or does not get shifted far enough to reach these extreme gears. The other work consists of cleaning, inspection and lubrication.

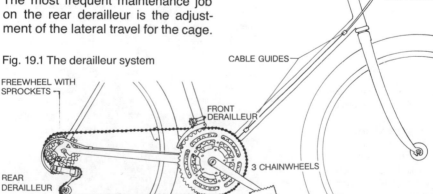

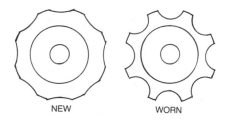

Fig. 19.3 New and worn derailleur pulleys

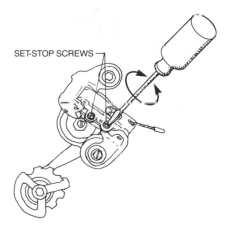

Fig. 19.4 Adjusting derailleur

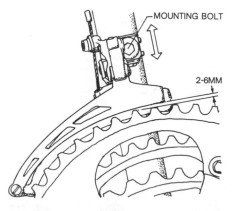

Fig. 19.5 Front derailleur

Clean the entire system after every demanding ride in dirty terrain or wet weather. Work a rag in between the cage and the pulleys as well as in the various other nooks and crannies, wrapping the rag around a narrow screwdriver to reach these tight spots. Replace any damaged or badly worn parts. Especially check the pulleys, of which Fig. 19.3 shows new and worn versions side by side. To adjust the derailleur, proceed as follows, using a small screwdriver. Proceed as follows:

### Adjust Rear Derailleur

1. Establish which form of adjustment is necessary. Note whether the chain is pushed too far or not far enough, on the inside for the low gear or on the outside for the high gear.
2. Set the rear derailleur in an intermediate gear by means of the shift lever, pedalling forward with the rear wheel raised off the ground.
3. The derailleur is equipped with two set-stop screws, usually marked with an L for low gear and an H for high gear adjustment. Tightening these screws restricts the derailleur's travel in the corresponding direction, loosening them expands it.
4. Using a small screwdriver as shown in Fig. 19.4, turn the appropriate screw in the necessary direction – about half a turn at a time. Repeat the operation, checking the result until you can change properly, without either overshifting or missing the extreme gear.

*Note:*
If it is impossible to achieve a satisfactory result, first check the movement of the shift lever and the cable, including its adjustment as explained below. Next, clean the cable and the mechanisms and lubricate the derailleur, using thin oil, such as WD-40 or the lightest grade of LPS. If still no luck, I suggest you take the bike to a bike shop for professional advice.

## The Front Derailleur

Shown in Fig. 19.5, the mountain bike's front derailleur, also called a changer, is a much simpler mechanism. It is attached to the seat tube just above the chainwheels and consists of a cage through which the chain is guided, attached to a simple hinge or parallelogram mechanism to move it sideways, carrying the chain over to the next chainring. No indexing here, at least not at the time of this writing: you move the shifter, pedalling all the while, until you notice that it shifts onto the next chainring, then back off a little to get it to run smoothly without scraping.

As far as maintenance is concerned, there is little to do here. Keep the mechanism clean and the pivots slightly lubricated. Make sure it is attached at the right height and with the cage parallel to the plane of the chainwheels. When you can't reach the extreme gear, or conversely overshift, dumping the chain, you should adjust the travel of the cage. That's done with the set-stop screws, following essentially the same procedure explained above for the rear derailleur.

## New Developments

Many new developments in bicycle componentry are introduced from time to time, though few seem to prove as useful as the manufacturers would have us believe. The most interesting and perfectly operating innovation that I have tried to date is the front gear system introduced by the Browning company. It is an electronically controlled unit on which the chain is not pushed sideways by a derailleur, but sections of the chainrings are hinged to pick up and deliver the chain to the next one. It works like a charm, even though I dislike the idea of electronically controlled, battery powered toys on my hitherto perfectly mechanical bicycle.

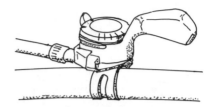
Fig. 19.6 Indexed shifter

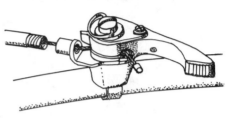
Fig. 19.7 Non-indexed shifter

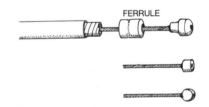
Fig. 19.8 Handlebar-end shifter

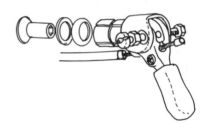
Fig. 19.9 Cable and nipple

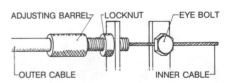
Fig. 19.10 Cable adjuster

## The Shifter Mechanism

Just about all mountain bikes these days are shifted by means of indexed thumb shifters mounted on the flat handlebars. To assure the most reliable and predictable shifting possible, make sure shifters and derailleurs are of the same make and model. At least one manufacturer offers a combination brake lever and shifter unit, which turns out to be less convenient, however elegant it looks. Only if the two levers are mounted separately, can you get both in the ergonomically optimum position to match *your* hand. Twist and turn the attachment until it is convenient to operate, whether changing to a higher or a lower gear, both front and rear.

I shall not bore you with the technical details hidden inside the shifters, which pull the derailleur cable in and out to shift the derailleur to the desired position. For the rear, it is a ratchet mechanism with a spring-tensioned pawl to arrest the lever in positions corresponding to the individual gears. The shifter for the front derailleur is a simple friction or non-indexed ratchet mechanism. The lever controlling the rear derailleur is mounted on the right, and the one for the front on the left.

The indexed shifters are equipped with a method of selecting the non-indexed mode, in case the indexing does not line up with the sprockets, resulting in scraping sounds and hesitant or unpredictable shifts. Fig. 19.6 shows an indexed, Fig. 19.7 a non-indexed shifter, designed for front and rear derailleur shifting, respectively.

Though that's the way virtually all mountain bikes are equipped, some of us incorrigibles install neither indexed shifters, nor flat wide bars, nor thumb shifters. What's perhaps more significant, at least two manufacturers equip their top notch mountain bikes this way, using slightly widened drop handlebars and the kind of bar-end shifters used on cyclo-cross racing bikes.

If you would like to try such an enigma that is even remotely affordable, check out the Bridgestone MB 1. To install bar-end shifters yourself, refer to Fig. 19.8. Route the cables along the handlebars, held with pieces of tape in some position where they don't get in your way, then cover the bars with the handlebar tape.

### Derailleur Cables

The shifters are connected to the derailleurs by means of flexible Bowden cables. The cable for the indexed rear derailleur should be relatively stiff and thick, also requiring a larger diameter outer cable. Fig. 19.9 shows the cable with its nipple, which is inserted at the shifter end, while the other end of the inner cable is clamped at the derailleur in an eye bolt or under a notched plate with a pinch bolt. Between the shifter and the derailleur, the cable is routed over and through guides mounted on the frame.

The revolutionary Browning front shifting mechanism. The chainwheel has a hinged section which literally picks up and delivers the chain to the other chainwheel.

## Cable Care

Remove the inner cables to clean them at least once a season. Lubricate the front derailleur cable with a rag soaked in vaseline or grease. The rear cable of an indexed system should be cleaned but not lubricated, to maintain adequate friction. At the same time, check to make sure there are no broken strands or frayed ends and that they run freely in the outer cables, which should not be pinched anywhere. Both inner and outer cables are cheap enough to replace if you're in doubt about their condition. Pull the cable taut with the derailleur and the lever both set for the smallest sprocket in the rear or the biggest chainring in the front, before tightening the pinch screw at the derailleur.

The tension of the derailleur cable may be adjusted when the shifting range can not be fully covered despite adjustment of the derailleur's set-stop screws. To do this, use the barrel adjuster shown in Fig. 19.10. Hold the barrel while loosening the locknut, then turn the adjuster in the appropriate direction to tighten or loosen, and finally hold the barrel while tightening the locknut again. Check operation of the gears, and readjust them if necessary.

# 20

# The Wheels

Nothing characterizes the mountain bike more than its fat tired wheels. While the typical ten-speed derailleur bike has tires that are at most one inch in width, those on mountain bikes can be anywhere from 1.5 to 2.2 inches. And those fat tires usually carry as pronounced a tread pattern as a pair of Vibram hiking boots. But apart from the sizes and a few other details, the mountain bike's wheels are much like those of any other bicycle.

A typical bicycle wheel is shown in Fig. 20.1. It is a spoked wheel with so-called wired-on tires. The latter consist of a separate inner tube and a cover that is held tight in a deep bedded metal rim by means of wire-reinforced beads. The other components of the wheel are hub and spokes. Wheel problems are perhaps the most common category of incidents, whether riding off-road or not, and

The hub forms the heart of the wheel. That makes this open heart surgery: the inner life of a SunTour mountain bike hub, showing cartridge bearings with double seals.

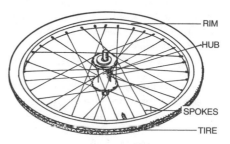

Fig. 20.1 Parts of the wheel

whether riding off-road or not, and their repair will be covered in some detail below.

### The Hub

The hub, shown in Fig. 20.2, forms the heart of the wheel. It may be either attached to fork or frame by means of a quick-release mechanism or by means of axle nuts. The former solution is often chosen for the front to allow easy wheel removal for transporting the bike. Though theoretically the solid axle used for wheels that are held with axle nuts is slightly stronger,

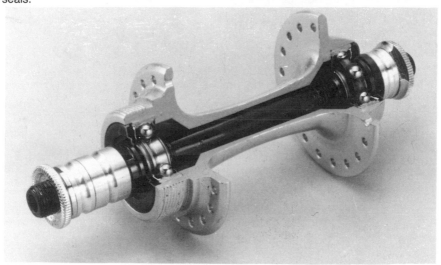

modern quick-release hubs have proven quite adequate for mountain bike use, certainly in the front. The preferable type of axle nuts are those with integral washers, shown in Fig. 20.3, while the quick release axle is shown in Fig. 20.4.

Fig. 20.5 shows a cross section of a typical hub. It consists of a hollow shell with flanges, to which the spokes are attached. The wheel axle is suspended on a set of bearings inside the hub shell. Bearings may be either of the adjustable type shown or non-adjustable cartridge bearings. Either way, they should be equipped with good dust seals for mountain bike use. The hub must have the same number of spoke holes as the rim, usually 36.

### Remove and Install Wheel

Taking the wheel out and putting it in is a matter of undoing the axle nuts or the quick-release. Though it's a very basic operation, it bears some instructions to do it effectively. In the case of a wheel with axle nuts, you need a matching wrench. For the rear wheel, you may need a rag to keep your hands clean while holding back the chain. Proceed as follows:

*Removal procedure:*
1. Either support the bike upright with the wheel off the ground, or turned upside-down, supported so that nothing on the handlebars gets damaged. When removing the rear wheel, select a gear with the smallest sprocket in the back and either the intermediate or the small chainwheel in the front, to minimize tension on the derailleur and the chain.
2. Loosen the axle nuts on both sides or undo the quick-release. The latter is loosened by twisting the lever into the 'open' position (see note below).

Fig. 20.2 The hub

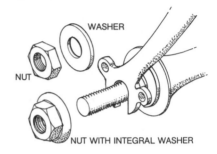

Fig. 20.3 Axle nut attachment

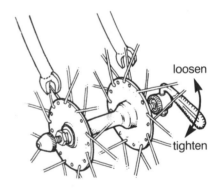

Fig. 20.4 Quick-release attachment

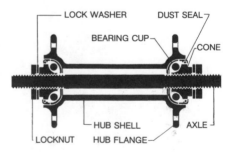

Fig. 20.5 Hub cross section

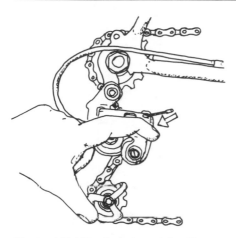

Fig. 20.6 Hold back chain and derailleur

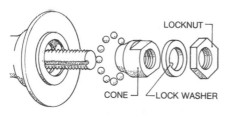

Fig. 20.7 Hub adjusting parts

3. Release or open the brake. On a cantilever or U-brake, that's done by removing one end of the straddle cable, on a cam-operated brake by twisting the cam plate out from between the rollers. With either type, you have to push the brake levers against the rim to release the cable tension while releasing the cable nipple or the cam plate.
4. Pull the wheel out. For the rear wheel, hold back the chain by means of the derailleur as shown in Fig. 20.6.

*Installation procedure:*
1. Take the preparatory action described under points 1, 2, and 3 under *Removal procedure* above.
2. Keep any brake parts out of the way while inserting the wheel, and hold back the derailleur on the rear wheel.

3. Align the wheel carefully, so it has the same clearance on both sides and the brake blocks match the sides of the rims when the brake arms are pushed together. Tighten the axle nuts or the quick-release lever (see note), while holding the wheel in the right position.

*Note:*
The quick-release is not opened or closed by unscrewing or tightening the thumb nut, but by twisting the lever in the appropriate direction to tighten or loosen the internal cam mechanism. Only if the wheel does not come out with the lever set in the 'open' position, should you loosen the thumb nut one or two turns, not forgetting to tighten it again when installing the wheel *before tightening the lever*.

### Hub Maintenance
Virtually all hubs bearing are packed with grease for lubrication. By and by, dirt and moisture enter the hub and mix with the grease, causing wear. The best way of lubricating the hub is to pour SAE 60 mineral oil through the oil hole in the hub, if it is so equipped. Catch excess oil in a basin under the hub, and dispose of it at a garage or gas station. If the hub has no oil hole, or if you don't like the mess this process makes, use grease for lubrication, and replace it at least once a year, following the instructions below.

When the hub bearings are too loose or too tight, it is time to lubricate and adjust the hub bearings. You will need an open-ended wrench and a set of cone wrenches in sizes to match the make and model of the hubs, purchased from a bike shop. Refer to Fig. 20.7, and proceed as follows after the wheel has been removed from the bike:

1. Loosen the locknut on one side, while holding the underlying cone

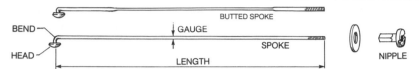

Fig. 20.8 The spokes

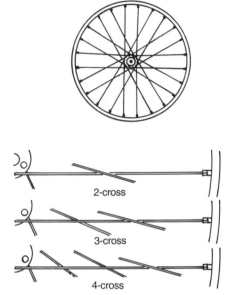

with one of the cone wrenches. When adjusting, back it off only two turns. Unscrew the locknut all the way to repack or overhaul the bearing.

2. To adjust, merely lift the lock washer a little, then adjust the cone relative to the opposite cone (to loosen) or the opposite locknut (to tighten).

3. To repack the bearings, remove lock washer and cone, after which the axle can be removed, catching the bearing balls. Clean and inspect everything, repack the cups with bearing grease and insert the bearing balls. Reassemble it in reverse order.

4. When the cone is adjusted so that the bearings turn freely without play, and the lock washer is in place, tighten the locknut, while holding the cone with the cone wrench.

5. Inspect the bearing once more. Tightness is most easily detected with the wheel removed, looseness with the wheel installed on the bike.

Fig. 20.9 Spoke crossing patterns

### The Spokes

The spokes, shown in Fig. 20.8, should be of stainless steel. Each spoke is held to the hub flange by its head to the rim by means of a screwed-on nipple. The latter should be kept tightened to maintain the spoke under tension. This actually prevents a lot of spoke breakage. The spokes run from the hub to the rim in one of several distinct patterns. Fig. 20.9 shows two, three and four-cross spoking patterns. The latter appears to be most suitable for the rear wheel, as it has been demonstrated to result in fewer spoke breakages.

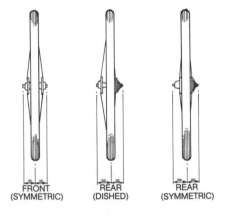

Fig. 20.10 Wheel centering

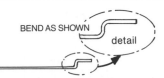

Fig. 20.11 Hooked spoke

The rim with the tire must be centered over the ends of the bearing locknuts. On the rear wheel, this normally creates a significant off-set relative to the hub flanges, due to the presence of the freewheel on the RH side. Fig. 20.10 shows several ways the wheel may be centered. The usual off-set in the rear wheel results in much higher forces on the spokes leading to the RH flange than in those on the other side of the wheel, which frequently leads to broken spokes on the RH side and makes it hard to keep the wheel trued. A noticeable improvement ensues when a special balanced hub is used in the rear, such as the Shimano Cassette Freehub, which has the freewheel built in, resulting in a more nearly equal spoke tension and fewer wheel problems.

The length of the spoke is measured as shown in Fig 20.8. It depends on the actual rim size, the type of hub and the spoking pattern. Make sure you know which sizes are needed for your wheels. They may be different for front and rear, and in the rear even for both sides. The strength is a function of the thickness – at least 2.0 mm (14 gauge or less) is the minimum required for a mountain bike. Butted spokes have a thinner section in the middle. They are as strong as regular spokes that are as thick as their thickest section (the lower gauge number in their size designation). If a spoke should brake, carry out a repair according to the following description:

## Replace Broken Spoke

1. Remove the freewheel, if the hole in the hub that corresponds to the broken spoke lies inaccessibly under the freewheel.
2. Remove the old spoke. If possible, unscrew the remaining section from the nipple, holding the latter with a wrench. If this is not possible, the tire must be deflated and locally lifted first, after which the nipple may be replaced by a new one.
3. Locate a spoke that runs the same way as the broken one: every fourth spoke along the circumference of the rim runs similarly. Check how it crosses the various other spokes that run the other way, using it as an example.
4. Thread the nipple on the spoke until it has the same tension as the other spokes of the wheel, or on the same side of the rear wheel.
5. If the spokes do not seem to be under enough tension, tighten all of them half a turn at a time, until they all seem equally taut and the wheel is reasonably true – if necessary, follow the instructions for *Wheel Truing* below to correct the situation.

*Note:*
For an emergency repair of the spokes on the RH side of the rear wheel, you may carry some special bent spokes, made from oversize spokes, bent according to Fig. 20.11 and hooked in the hub flange without removing the freewheel. Take the bike to a bike shop to get these provisional spokes replaced as soon as possible. You can also do it yourself, after removing the freewheel following the instruction in Chapter 18.

## The Rim

Fig. 20.12 shows typical rim cross sections. For a mountain bike of any quality, the rims must be aluminum, which is reasonably light and strong. In addition, the aluminum surface provides much better braking when wet than the chrome plating used on steel rims. The rim should match the tire, which will be discussed below. For mountain bike use very strong rims that are heavier than those used on ten-speeds are selected. The trend in recent years has been towards narrower rims. Right now, the universally preferred mountain bike rim seems to be 20 mm wide (measured inside). Stronger models tend to be those that are a little heavier, but well worth the extra weight.

The spoke holes in the rim should be reinforced by means of ferrules. To protect the tube, a piece of tape should cover the part of the rim bed where the spoke nipples would otherwise touch the inner tube.

## Wheel Truing

If the wheel is bent, which may or may not be the result of a broken spoke, proceed as follows to straighten it by retensioning certain spokes, as shown in Fig. 20.13:

1. Establish where it is offset to the left, where to the right, by turning it slowly while watching at a fixed reference point, such as the brake shoes. Mark the relevant sections.
2. Tighten LH spokes in the area where the rim is off-set to the RH side, while loosening the ones on the LH ones – and vice versa.
3. Repeat steps 1 and 2 several times, until the wheel is true enough not to rub on the brakes. This will get you by but, unless you are quite good at it, I suggest you get the job done properly by a bike mechanic as soon as possible.

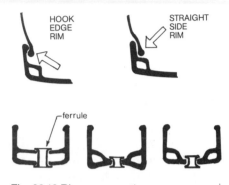

Fig. 20.12 Rim cross sections

## The Tires

The size of the tire defines the nominal size of the wheel. Adult mountain bikes usually have 26 inch wheels with tires that may vary from 1.5 to 2.2 inches in width. These nominal sizes don't necessarily coincide exactly with the actual dimensions. To give an example, 26 inch tires normally measure as big in circumference as some tires referred to as 700 mm, although 700 mm would be more like 28 inches.

It all depends on the tire cross section or width. The rim for a mountain bike tire has a rim bed diameter of 559 mm. Add to that twice the actual tire cross section, and you have the tire's outside diameter, illustrated in Fig. 20.14. This is the ETRTO tire designation system, worked out by the European tire and rim manufacturers association and adopted by the ISO international standard system. Unfortunately, this system is largely ignored by US and oriental manufacturers, who seem to prefer bewildering their customers with designations that bear little reference to the actual dimensions.

As for the recommended tire width, it all depends on the terrain encountered. The minimum width suitable for any kind of off-road cycling is probably 47 mm (1.75 in), while 59 mm (2.2 in) is the cat's whiskers for both very soft and very rocky ground. The

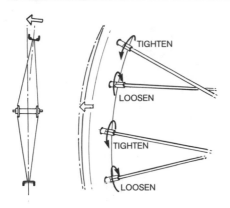

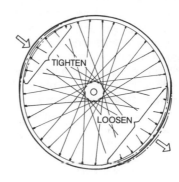

Fig. 20.13 Wheel truing

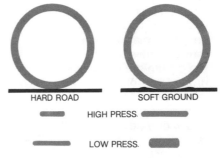

HARD ROAD          SOFT GROUND

HIGH PRESS.

LOW PRESS.

Fig. 20.15 Tire contact area

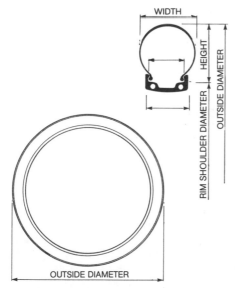

Fig. 20.14 Wheel and tire dimensions

1.5 and 1.6 in tires found on cheaper imports are a compromise to the exorbitant excise tax initiated in the thirties to protect US industry, though they may be fine if you only ride on paved roads.

Most people have the mistaken belief that a tire's rolling resistance necessarily increases with its width. Actually, the rolling resistance of a tire is a function of the extent to which the tire or the road deform at their contact area. Fig. 20.15 illustrates this. Clearly, on a smooth hard road, the only way to fly is with a tire that is inflated really hard. On soft or rocky ground, on the other hand, that tire had better be a little softer.

Soft ground calls for pressures of no more than 25 psi (1.7 bar) at low speeds, a little higher at higher speeds. On smooth asphalt or other smooth hard surfaces, you may go all the way to 75 psi (6 bar) for high speed cycling. All other combinations lie somewhere in between. Experiment with tire pressures for different kinds of riding, frequently checking with a tire pressure gauge, until you have developed a feel for the pressure that is best for certain conditions.

To judge a new tire before buying, note that a light and flexible model, that stretches as shown in Fig. 20.16 and has easily deformable sidewalls, tends to have better running characteristics. Select a diameter, a weight and a tread pattern that matches your needs.

Fig. 20.18 depicts three different thread patterns. What will be best for you depends on where and how you ride. The very knobby tires that are characteristic of early mountain bikes are still ideal for off-road cycling, especially on soft ground or snow. Knobs that are offset relative to one another, so that distinct interruptions are formed between rows of knobs along the circumference, provide best soft-ground traction. Patterns on which the knobs are offset in a continuous pattern provide less rolling resistance. The widely advertised patterns with a raised center ridge provide neither good traction nor particularly low rolling resistance – and they handle unpredictably in curves.

The perfectly smooth tires, called slicks, that are slowly becoming available for mountain bikes as well as for ten-speeds, work fine on regular roads and hard rocky surfaces, even when it is wet. They work best when inflated, since the pressure between tire and road is proportional to the inflation pressure, and the higher this pressure, the more chance water is pushed out from under the tire, which is essential for good contact.

For icy conditions, there are studded tires. The Finnish Nokia company has made them as long as I can remember – these are available in Britain. These studded tires are presently available only in versions to match the European 650 mm wheels with the larger diameter 584 mm rim. This may require the brakes to be

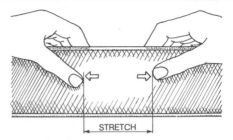

Fig. 20.16 Tire flex test

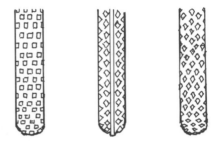

Fig. 20.17 Tire tread patterns

installed in a different location, unless they are adjustable over an unusually wide range. More recently, IRC has introduced its studded Blizzard tire in the US, which is available in a size to match the standard 559 mm mountain bike rim.

**Tube and Valve**

The inner tube is inflated by means of a valve, several types of which are illustrated in Fig. 20.18. By far the most suitable is the Presta valve, since it requires much less force to inflate properly. Unscrew the round nut at the tip before inflating, and tighten it again afterwards. Unfortunately, Presta valves can't be inflated with a gas station air hose, unless you have an adaptor nipple. And even if you do, chances are the thing leaks air. This is the reason most manufacturers install tires with the cruder Schrader valves used on car tires.

The tube should preferably match the size of the tire, although most tubes stretch enough to go anywhere

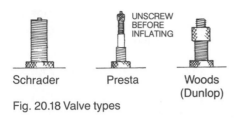

Schrader          Presta          Woods
                                 (Dunlop)

Fig. 20.18 Valve types

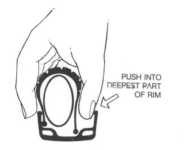

Fig. 20.19 Push tire into rim bed

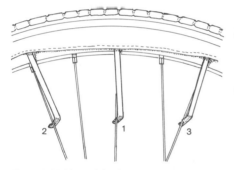

Fig. 20.20 Use of tire irons

from 1.5 to 1.9 in or from 1.75 to 2.2 in cross section, respectively. The lowest rolling resistance is offered by the lightest and most flexible tubes. Thin latex tubes are the lightest and provide the lowest rolling resistance. Use them only for tires that have about the same nominal cross section since they don't hold the air properly if stretched too much. At the other extreme, very thick butyl tubes lend themselves to terrain with thorns and other tiny, sharp objects. They offer little advantage in other conditions, since the typical flat is not caused by a penetrating pointed item, but in the sidewall area when the tube gets pinched between the rim and a hard object.

### Fixing a Flat

Sooner or later, every cyclist gets a flat, and you should be able to handle this repair yourself. Carry a puncture kit, three tire irons (called tyre levers in Britain), a pump and perhaps a spare tube. The adhesive quality of the patches in your kit deteriorates over time, so I suggest replacing them once a year. Proceed as follows:

1. Remove the wheel from the bike. On a rear wheel, first select the gear with the small chainwheel and sprocket, then hold the chain with the derailleur back as shown in Fig 20.6 at the beginning of this chapter.
2. Check whether the cause is visible from the outside. If so, remove it and mark its location, so you know where to work.
3. Remove the valve cap and unscrew the round nut (if you have a Presta valve); then remove the locknut at the base of the valve stem, if installed.
4. Push the valve body in and work one side of the tire into the deeper center of the rim, as shown in Fig. 20.19.
5. Put a tire iron under the bead on that side, at some distance from the valve, then use it to lift the bead over the rim edge and hook it on a spoke, as shown in Fig. 20.20.
6. Do the same with the second tire iron two spokes to the left and with the third one two spokes to the right. Now the first one will come loose, so you may use it in a fourth location, if necessary.
7. When enough of the tire sidewall is lifted over the rim, you can lift the rest over by hand.

8. Remove the tube, saving the valve until last, when it must be pushed back through the valve hole in the rim.
9. Try inflating the tire and check where air escapes. If the hole is very small, so it isn't easily detected, pass the tube slowly past your eye, which is quite sensitive. If still no luck, dip the tube under water, a section at a time: the hole is wherever bubbles escape. Mark its location and dry the tire if appropriate. Check the whole tube, since there may be more than one hole.
10. Make sure the area around the patch is dry and clean, then roughen it with sand paper or the scraper from the puncture kit and remove the resulting dust. Treat an area slightly larger than the patch you want to use.
11. Spread a thin, even film of rubber solution on the treated area. Let dry about 3 minutes.
12. Remove the foil backing from the patch, without touching the adhesive side. Place it with the adhesive side down on the treated area, centered over the hole. Apply pressure over the entire patch to improve adhesion.
13. Sprinkle talcum powder from the patch kit over the treated area.
14. Inflate the tube to a moderate pressure and wait long enough to make sure the repair is carried out properly.
15. Meanwhile, check the inside of the tire and remove any sharp objects that may have caused the puncture. Also make sure no spoke ends are projecting from the rim bed – file flush if necessary and cover with rim tape.
16. Let enough air out of the tube to make it limp but not completely empty. Then reinsert it under the tire, starting at the valve.
17. Pull the tire back over the edge of the rim without using a tool. Start opposite the valve, which must be done last. If it seems too tight, force the part already installed deeper into the center of the rim bed, working around towards the valve from both sides.
18. Make sure the tube is not pinched between the rim and the tire bead anywhere, working and kneading the tire sidewall until the tube is free.
19. Inflate the tire to about a third its final pressure.
20. Center the tire relative to the rim, making sure it lies evenly all around on both sides, then install the locknut.
21. Inflate it to the final pressure, then install the wheel. If the tire is wider than the rim, you may have to release the brake – and tighten it again afterwards. For the rear wheel, hold back the chain with the derailleurs set for a small chainwheel and a small sprocket.

*Note:*
If the valve leaks, or if the tube is seriously damaged, the entire tube must be replaced, which is done following the relevant steps of these same instructions. Replacement of the tire cover is done similarly. Always make sure the rim tape that covers the spoke ends is intact.

# 21
# The Brakes

Your mountain bike's brakes are important, though not just for coming to a sudden halt. Consider what happens when you come thundering down a steep slope, heading straight for a giant sequoia or whatever clutters the backwoods in your part of the world. You have four choices: run into the obstacle, ride around it, stop before you get there or some combination of the latter two. Usually, you will use the last option, slowing down to a lower speed, at which you can safely divert to avoid the obstacle. But whatever you do, you need brakes.

Technically seen, whether slowing down or coming to a complete halt, you have to decelerate the bike. There's a lot of kinetic energy stored in the moving mass of bike and rider.

Shimano Deore U-brake with matching brake handle. Though the U-brake is usually installed in the back, some manufacturers also put this thing in the front,

The brakes are used to dissipate some of that energy. If you did not dissipate the energy by braking, you'd eventually do it by hitting the obstacle – with disastrous results.

In practice, two forms of braking can be distinguished: to regulate speed gently or to come to a sudden stop. Speed regulation is usually the more demanding, since it requires more feeling. Whatever form of braking is practiced, the kinetic energy of the moving mass is transformed into heat.

The amount of heat generated while slowing down gradually or stopping suddenly on a long steep downhill is quite substantial. The predecessor of the modern mountain bike used to be equipped with a coaster brake, also known as back-pedalling brake, built into the hub of the rear wheel. If you take a look at one of those and consult a high school physics text,

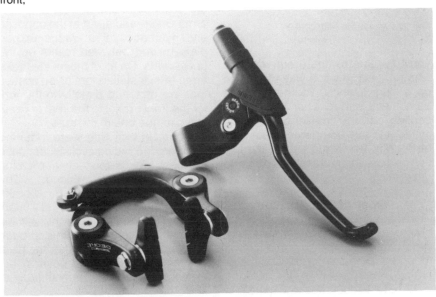

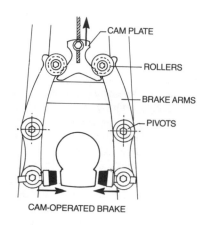

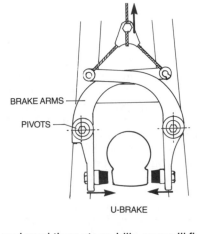

CAM-OPERATED BRAKE

U-BRAKE

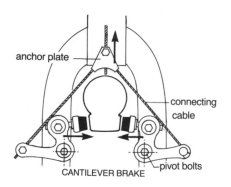

Fig. 21.1 Mountain bike brakes

you'll be able to figure out why that was not such a good way of braking on a long downhill. You need lots of bare metal surfaces for friction and cooling, and the coaster brake is tiny inside and out, compared to the area of the rim, which represents the friction and cooling surface on a bike with rim brakes.

## Types of Rim Brakes

There are three different types of rim brakes suitable for mountain bikes: the cantilever brake, the pivot-mounted roller-cam brake and the U-brake. These three types are depicted in Fig. 21.1. In countries with more rain

and mud than steep hills, you will find mountain bikes equipped with hub brakes. In the US, these are rare enough to be ignored here – you will find instructions for handling such brakes in my *Bicycle Repair Book* in case you are interested.

On all rim brakes, a pair of brake blocks is pushed against the sides of the rim when the brake is applied. On the cantilever and U-brake, this is done via a cantilever system pulled together with a connecting cable. On the roller-cam brake, the cantilever arms are spread apart at the opposite end by means of a wedge-shaped plate guided between rollers on the brake arms. On all of these, the brake arms are installed on pivot bosses that are attached directly to the fork for the front brake, to the seat or chain stays for the one in the rear.

Mountain bike riders are fortunate compared to racing cyclists, because the best brakes for their application are reasonably priced. The paramount criterion for a good brake is that it must be rigid, while still opening up far enough to clear the fat tires. All three designs allow this, though you must ascertain whether the pivot bosses are installed in a position that allows the use of the particular brake selected.

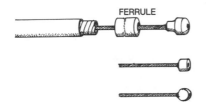

Fig. 21.2 Cable and nipples

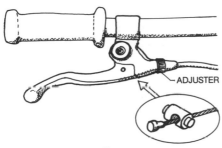

Fig. 21.3 Brake handle

When comparing different versions of the same basic system, look for a type that provides maximum rigidity and smooth operation. Amongst cantilever brakes, the Shimano Deore models, with their triangulated cantilevers, are my favorites. The latest version of the SunTour Powercam, which has a powerful centering spring, is the ultimate brake amongst non-cantilevers. U-brakes and cam-operated models have the advantage that they do not project as far as the cantilever brake.

### Brake Controls

With any rim brake, the force applied by pulling the lever is transmitted to the brake unit by means of flexible Bowden cables, shown in Fig. 21.2. These cables are partly contained in flexible outer cables and restrained at anchor points on the frame. The force is transmitted to the part of the brake unit to which the cable is attached. A

pivoting action then pulls or pushes the ends of the brake arms with the brake blocks against the sides of the rim to create the drag that slows down the bike.

The brake handle, a typical one of which is shown in Fig. 21.3, should also be designed very rigidly. It must work smoothly and be easy to reach, while allowing full application of the brake, leaving about 2 cm (¾ in) clearance between the handlebars and the lever. The type of levers designed for mountain bikes are quite suitable for any bike with flat handlebars, providing the attachment clamp matches the bar diameter. If you like to use drop handlebars, you will need normal racing brake levers. Amongst these, models with extension levers are not satisfactory, since they are not rigid enough.

SunTour XC roller cam brake. The wedge shaped plate is pulled up to separate the rollers at the top of the brake arms, pushing the brake blocks against the rim, when the brake lever is applied.

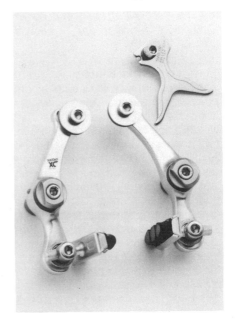

All rim brakes have an adjustment mechanism to shorten the cable, which allows you to take up any slack in the cable. Though all mountain bike handles have such an adjuster integrated, there may be an additional one at one of the cable anchor points. If you use a drop bar with racing levers, this will be your only adjuster. The adjustment is described below. Some brakes have a quick-release mechanism to allow easy wheel removal and installation, without affecting adjustment of the brake. If not, they can be loosened by pushing the brake blocks against the rim and at the same time removing the connecting cable on the cantilever or U-brake, or the cam plate on the roller-cam brake, respectively.

Brake cables should not be elastic or 'spungy' to allow applying adequate force. Relatively thick, preferably stainless steel, inner cables and non-compressing outer cables with a PTFE or other low-friction liner are best for use with any make or model of brake. Brake cables should be routed as short as possible, providing they are not forced into excessively tight bends in any position of the handlebars.

### Brake Blocks

The brake blocks should be of a composition material that provides adequate friction even in the rain, which is not the case with plain rubber brake blocks. Contrary to popular belief, longer brake blocks are not necessarily better. Though they may last longer, they actually provide poorer braking than shorter ones, given the same material. This is due to the fact that the pressure, and thus the ability to remove water, between the brake block and the rim is greater for a smaller brake block, since the pressure is the quotient of the force – which is the same in both cases – di-

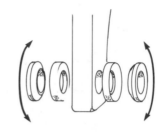

Fig. 21.4 Brake block installation

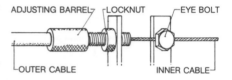

Fig. 21.5 Adjuster mechanism

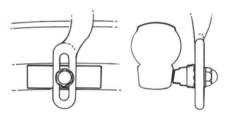

Fig. 21.6 Brake block alignment

Fig. 21.7 Adjuster at brake handle

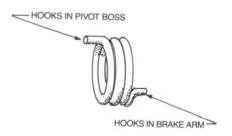

Fig. 21.8 Brake lever return spring

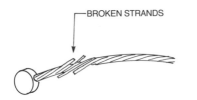

Fig. 21.9 Frayed cable

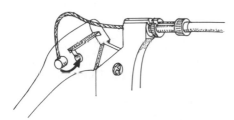

Fig. 21.10 Nipple in brake handle

vided by the area. Typically, mountain bike brake blocks, or rather the holders or shoes in which they are held, can be adjusted in all three planes by means of some combination of spherical and dished surfaces, an example of which is shown in Fig. 21.4.

### Brake Check

To make sure the brakes work reliably, check whether they are attached properly and then test them at low speed. Try them out separately at walking speed, which is perfectly safe and still gives a representative test of the deceleration reached with each brake when travelling at speed. Used alone while riding the bike, the rear brake must be strong enough to skid the wheel when applied firmly. The front brake should decelerate the bike so that the rider feels the rear wheel lifting off when it is fully applied. If their performance is inadequate, carry out the adjustment described below.

### Adjust Brake

We will assume the brake must be adjusted because its performance is insufficient. In this case, the cable ten-

sion must be increased by decreasing its length. Should the brake touch the rim even when not engaged, the opposite must be done to lengthen the cable slightly. The adjuster mechanism is shown in Fig. 21.5.

Before starting, check to make sure the brake blocks lie on the rim properly over their entire width and length when the brake is applied, as shown in Fig. 21.6. Ideally, the front of the brake block should touch the rim just a little earlier than the back. If necessary, adjust by loosening the brake block bolt, moving the block as appropriate. Retighten it while holding the brake block in the right position. If necessary, the brake block may be replaced. Proceed as follows:

1. Release brake quick-release if installed.
2. Loosen the locknut on the adjusting mechanism for the brake cable, which on mountain bikes is usually installed on the brake handle, shown in Fig. 21.7.
3. While holding the locknut, screw the barrel adjuster out by several turns; then tighten the quick-release again, if your brake has one.
4. Check the brake tension: the brake must grab the rim firmly when a minimum of 2 cm (¾ in) clearance remains between the brake handle and the handlebars.
5. If necessary, repeat steps 1 through 4 until the brake works properly.
6. Tighten the locknut again, while holding the adjusting barrel to stop it from turning.

### Center Brake

If the brake drags on the rim on one side, while the other side is still some distance away, the unit must be centered. Regardless whether you have cantilever, cam-operated or U-brakes, this is done by bending the springs on the pivots in or out a little. A typical example of such a spring is shown Fig. 21.8. This job can only be done by disassembling the unit, after establishing which pivot spring has to be tightened or opened a little. Use two thin pliers to bend the spring into the required shape. Reassemble and check again – repeat if necessary.

### Replace Brake Cable

To avoid the unsettling experience of brake cable snapping just when it is most needed, I suggest you replace it as soon as individual strands show signs of damage at the end nipple, as shown in Fig. 21.9. Since a cable may have to be replaced while you are away from home, it will be smart to carry a spare. Make sure the spare cable has a nipple that matches the particular brake handle used on your bike. Proceed as follows:

1. Loosen the brake quick-release, if installed, or squeeze the brake arms together, removing the cam plate on the roller cam brake or the straddle cable on other types of mountain bike brake.
2. Loosen the eye bolt that holds the cable at the brake anchor plate, until you can pull the old cable out.
3. Push the old cable out, working towards the handle, where you can dislodge the nipple as shown in Fig. 21.10, after turning the locknut until its slot lines up with the one in the barrel adjuster. Then pull the entire inner cable out, catching the outer cable section or sections, as well as any other parts, memorizing their installation locations.
4. Lubricate the new cable with grease or vaseline. Back off on the locknut, then screw the adjusting barrel in all the way.
5. Starting at the handle, push the new cable through, securing the nipple by pulling it taut. Thread the inner cable through the various anchor points, outer cable sections and other parts. Finally push it through the eye bolt or the pinch plate at the brake.
6. Locate the nipple into the handle, then pull the cable taut from the brake end and tighten the eye bolt or pinch bolt, using tools with enough leverage on both parts of the screwed connection.
7. Adjust the cable tension, following the preceding instruction.

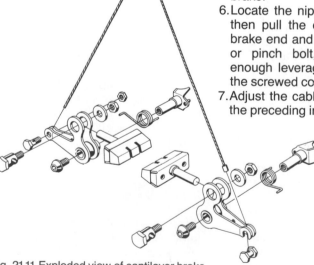

Fig. 21.11 Exploded view of cantilever brake

8. Test the brake in operation, followed by a final adjustment if necessary.
9. Finally, cut off the free end of cable until about 3 cm (1¼ in) projects, using sharp cutters.

## Overhaul Brakes

Sometimes you may find that no amount of adjusting solves your brake problems. In that case, it is time to overhaul the mechanism. Refer to the exploded views Fig. 21.11, Fig. 21.12 and Fig. 21.13 for cantilever, cam-operated and U-brake, respectively. Proceed systematically, taking the lever,

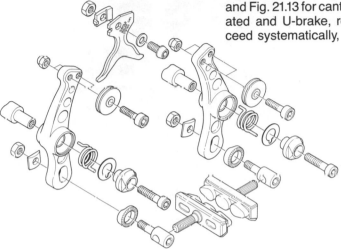

Fig. 21.12 Exploded view of cam-operated brake

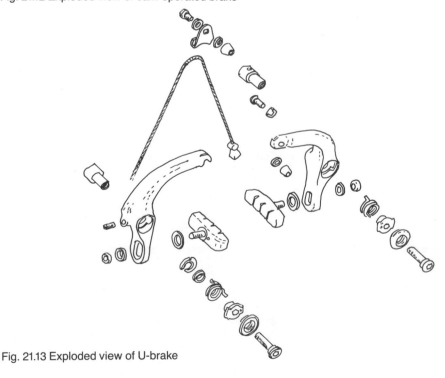

Fig. 21.13 Exploded view of U-brake

Shimano Deore XT
cantilever brakes.

the brake mechanism, and the cable one at a time. Disassemble, inspect, clean, lubricate and rebuild the items the way they were originally. Replace any parts that are beyond repair. I have included exploded view draw- ings of some typical assemblies for your guidance. Do use your own imagination a little, and try to estab- lish along the way what may be the problem. Take the bike to a bike shop if you can't solve it yourself.

# Appendix

## Table 1. Frame sizing table

| leg length | | recommended seat tube height | | | | recommended straddle height ground to top tube | |
| --- | --- | --- | --- | --- | --- | --- | --- |
| | | A center to top of lug | | B center-to-center | | | |
| cm | in | cm | in | cm | in | cm | in |
| 72 |    | 43 | 16.5 | 41 | 16   | 60 |    |
| 73 | 29 | 45 | 17   | 43 | 16.5 | 61 | 23 |
| 74 |    | 46 | 17.5 | 44 | 17   | 62 |    |
| 75 |    | 46 | 17.5 | 44 | 17   | 62 |    |
| 76 | 30 | 47 | 18   | 45 | 17.5 | 63 | 25 |
| 77 |    | 48 | 18.5 | 46 | 18   | 64 |    |
| 78 |    | 49 | 19   | 47 | 18   | 66 |    |
| 79 | 31 | 50 | 19.5 | 48 | 18.5 | 67 | 26 |
| 80 |    | 51 | 20   | 49 | 19   | 68 |    |
| 81 | 32 | 52 | 21   | 50 | 19.5 | 69 | 27 |
| 82 |    | 53 | 21   | 51 | 20   | 70 |    |
| 83 |    | 54 | 21.5 | 52 | 20.5 | 71 |    |
| 84 | 33 | 55 | 21.5 | 53 | 21   | 72 | 28 |
| 85 |    | 56 | 22   | 54 | 21.5 | 73 |    |
| 86 | 34 | 57 | 22.5 | 55 | 22   | 74 | 29 |
| 87 |    | 58 | 22.5 | 56 | 22   | 75 |    |
| 88 |    | 59 | 23   | 57 | 22.5 | 76 | 30 |
| 89 | 35 | 60 | 23.5 | 58 | 23   | 77 |    |
| 90 |    | 61 | 24   | 59 | 23.5 | 78 |    |
| 91 | 36 | 62 | 24.5 | 60 | 23.5 | 81 | 32 |
| 92 |    | 63 | 24.5 | 61 | 24   | 82 |    |

*Remarks:*
The seat tube lengths shown in this table are recommended values. The maximum size is about one inch (2.5 cm) more, the minimum about one inch (2.5 cm) less.

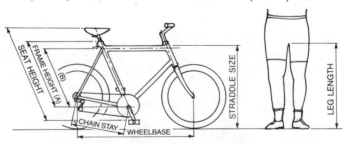

## Table 2.  Conversion between gear numbers  and development

Gear number (inches)

| 30 | 40 | 50 | 60 | 70 | 80 | 90 | 100 | 110 | 120 |

| 2.0 | 3.0 | 4.0 | 5.0 | 6.0 | 7.0 | 8.0 | 10.0 | 11.0 |

Development (meters)

**Table 3. Gear table for 26-in wheels**

Number of teeth on chainwheel

| Sprocket | 24 | 26 | 28 | 30 | 32 | 34 | 36 | 38 | 39 | 40 | 41 | 42 | 43 | 44 | 45 | 46 | 47 | 48 | 49 | 50 | 51 | 52 | 53 | |
|---|---|---|---|---|---|---|---|---|---|---|---|---|---|---|---|---|---|---|---|---|---|---|---|---|
| 13 | 48 | 52 | 56 | 60 | 64 | 68 | 72 | 76 | 78 | 80 | 82 | 84 | 86 | 88 | 90 | 92 | 94 | 96 | 98 | 100 | 102 | 104 | 106 | 13 |
| 14 | 45 | 48 | 52 | 56 | 60 | 63 | 67 | 70 | 72 | 74 | 76 | 78 | 80 | 82 | 84 | 85 | 87 | 89 | 91 | 93 | 95 | 97 | 98 | 14 |
| 15 | 42 | 45 | 49 | 52 | 55 | 59 | 62 | 66 | 68 | 69 | 71 | 73 | 75 | 76 | 78 | 80 | 81 | 83 | 85 | 87 | 88 | 90 | 92 | 15 |
| 16 | 39 | 42 | 45 | 49 | 52 | 55 | 58 | 61 | 63 | 65 | 67 | 68 | 70 | 72 | 73 | 75 | 76 | 78 | 80 | 81 | 83 | 85 | 86 | 16 |
| 17 | 37 | 40 | 43 | 46 | 49 | 52 | 55 | 58 | 60 | 61 | 63 | 64 | 66 | 67 | 69 | 70 | 72 | 73 | 75 | 76 | 78 | 80 | 81 | 17 |
| 18 | 35 | 38 | 40 | 43 | 46 | 49 | 52 | 55 | 56 | 58 | 59 | 61 | 62 | 64 | 65 | 66 | 68 | 69 | 71 | 72 | 74 | 75 | 77 | 18 |
| 19 | 33 | 36 | 38 | 41 | 44 | 47 | 49 | 52 | 53 | 55 | 56 | 57 | 59 | 60 | 62 | 63 | 64 | 66 | 67 | 68 | 70 | 71 | 73 | 19 |
| 20 | 31 | 34 | 36 | 39 | 42 | 44 | 47 | 49 | 51 | 52 | 53 | 55 | 56 | 57 | 59 | 60 | 61 | 62 | 64 | 65 | 66 | 68 | 69 | 20 |
| 21 | 30 | 32 | 35 | 37 | 40 | 42 | 45 | 47 | 48 | 50 | 51 | 52 | 53 | 54 | 56 | 57 | 58 | 59 | 61 | 62 | 63 | 64 | 66 | 21 |
| 22 | 28 | 31 | 33 | 35 | 38 | 40 | 43 | 45 | 46 | 47 | 48 | 50 | 51 | 52 | 53 | 54 | 56 | 57 | 58 | 59 | 60 | 61 | 63 | 22 |
| 23 | 27 | 29 | 32 | 34 | 36 | 38 | 41 | 43 | 44 | 45 | 46 | 47 | 49 | 50 | 51 | 52 | 53 | 54 | 55 | 57 | 58 | 59 | 60 | 23 |
| 24 | 26 | 28 | 30 | 32 | 35 | 37 | 39 | 41 | 42 | 43 | 44 | 45 | 47 | 48 | 49 | 50 | 51 | 52 | 53 | 54 | 55 | 56 | 57 | 24 |
| 25 | 25 | 27 | 29 | 31 | 33 | 35 | 37 | 39 | 41 | 42 | 43 | 44 | 45 | 46 | 47 | 48 | 49 | 50 | 51 | 52 | 53 | 54 | 55 | 25 |
| 26 | 24 | 26 | 28 | 30 | 32 | 34 | 36 | 38 | 39 | 40 | 41 | 42 | 43 | 44 | 45 | 46 | 47 | 48 | 49 | 50 | 51 | 52 | 53 | 26 |
| 27 | 23 | 25 | 27 | 29 | 31 | 33 | 35 | 37 | 38 | 39 | 39 | 40 | 41 | 42 | 43 | 44 | 45 | 46 | 47 | 48 | 49 | 50 | 51 | 27 |
| 28 | 22 | 24 | 26 | 28 | 30 | 32 | 33 | 35 | 36 | 37 | 38 | 39 | 40 | 41 | 42 | 43 | 44 | 45 | 46 | 46 | 47 | 48 | 49 | 28 |
| 30 | 21 | 23 | 24 | 26 | 28 | 29 | 31 | 33 | 34 | 35 | 36 | 36 | 37 | 38 | 39 | 40 | 41 | 42 | 42 | 43 | 44 | 45 | 46 | 30 |
| 32 | 20 | 21 | 23 | 24 | 26 | 28 | 29 | 31 | 32 | 33 | 33 | 34 | 35 | 35 | 37 | 37 | 38 | 39 | 40 | 41 | 41 | 42 | 43 | 32 |
| 34 | 18 | 20 | 21 | 23 | 24 | 26 | 28 | 29 | 30 | 31 | 31 | 32 | 33 | 33 | 34 | 35 | 36 | 37 | 37 | 38 | 39 | 40 | 41 | 34 |
| 38 | 16 | 18 | 19 | 21 | 22 | 23 | 25 | 26 | 27 | 27 | 28 | 29 | 29 | 30 | 31 | 31 | 32 | 32 | 33 | 34 | 35 | 36 | 36 | 38 |
| | 24 | 26 | 28 | 30 | 32 | 34 | 36 | 38 | 39 | 40 | 41 | 42 | 43 | 44 | 45 | 46 | 47 | 48 | 49 | 50 | 51 | 52 | 53 | |

Number of teeth on sprocket

See Chapter 6 for the derivation of the formula and additional explanations.

## Troubleshooting guide

| Problem/symptom | Possible cause | Required correction | For description see |
|---|---|---|---|
| bike hard to ride (high resistance when coasting and pedalling) | 1. insufficient tire pressure | inflate and/or mend tire (use high-pressure pump) | chapter 20 (tires) chapter 4 (pump) |
| | 2. wheel rubs on brake, fork or frame | adjust brake; adjust or straighten wheel; install narrower tire if insufficient clearance | chapter 16 (wheel) chapter 20 (brake) |
| | 3. dirt build-up on wheel or bike | clean bike | chapter 2 |
| | 4. resistance in wheel bearings | lubricate, adjust or overhaul wheel bearings | chapter 20 |
| bike hard to pedal (but coasts alright) | 1. accumulated dirt on chain | clean chain, chainwheels, sprockets and derailleurs | chapters 2, 18, 19 |
| | 2. insufficient lubrication on chain | lubricate | chapter 18 |
| | 3. resistance in bottom bracket or pedal bearings | lubricate, adjust or overhaul bearings | chapter 18 |
| chain drops off chain-wheel or sprocket | 1. derailleur out of adjustment | adjust derailleurs | chapter 19 |
| gears do not engage properly | 1. shift lever dirty, loose or defective | clean, adjust, lubricate or replace | chapters 2 and 19 |
| | 2. derailleur cable anchor or guides loose, or cable corroded | tighten attachments or replace cable | chapter 19 |
| | 3. derailleur out of adjustment | adjust derailleur | chapter 19 |
| | 4. chain too short or too long | correct or replace | chapter 18 |

| Problem | Cause | Solution | Reference |
|---|---|---|---|
| inadequate braking | 1. rim or brake wet, greasy or dirty | clean rim and brake | chapters 2, 20, 21 |
| | 2. brakes out of adjustment | adjust brakes | chapter 21 |
| | 3. friction in brake cables | replace or lubricate | chapter 21 |
| | 4. brake shoe worn | replace brake shoe | chapter 21 |
| brakes squeak | 1. brake attachment loose | adjust and tighten | chapter 21 |
| | 2. brake pad worn | replace | chapter 21 |
| | 3. rim or brake pad dirty | clean or replace pad | chapters 2 and 21 |
| | (if none of these causes: don't worry, some brakes just squeak) | | |
| chain slips | 1. chain and sprockets dirty | clean and lubricate | chapters 2 and 18 |
| | 2. rear derailleur out of adjustment | adjust | chapter 19 |
| | 3. chain worn (especially when used with new freewheel) | replace chain | chapter 18 |
| | 4. freewheel sprocket worn | replace sprocket or freewheel | chapter 18 |
| irregular pedalling movement | 1. crank or pedal loose | tighten cranks and pedals | chapter 18 |
| | 2. pedal or bottom bracket bearing out of adjustment | adjust or overhaul | chapter 18 |
| | 3. crank, chainwheel or pedal axle bent | replace or get straightened | see bike shop |
| steering vibrates or is inprecise | 1. wheels out of true or not in line | center and true both wheels and, if necessary, get frame and fork aligned | chapter 20 / see bike shop |
| | 2. head-set bearings loose or worn | adjust, overhaul or replace | chapter 15 |
| | 3. wheel bearings loose | adjust or overhaul | chapter 20 |

# Addresses

Australian Cycling Council
153 The Kingsway
Cronulla
Sydney 2230
Australia

Bicycle Federation of America
1818 R St. N.W.
Washington, DC 20009
USA

Bicycle Federation of Australia
399 Pitt Street
Sydney 2000
Australia

Bicycle USA
League of American Wheelmen
Suite 209
6707 Whitestone Road
Baltimore, MD 21207
USA

Bikecentennial
Box 8308
Missoula, MT 59807
USA

British Cycling Federation
70 Brompton Road
London SW3 1EN
Great Britain

British Cycling Federation
Touring Bureau
3 Moor Lane
Lancaster
Great Britain

Bureau of Land Management
US Department of the Interior
18th and C Streets, NW
Room 1013
Washington, DC 20240

Canadian Cycling Association
Touring Department
333 River Road
Vanier, Ontario KIL 8B9
Canada

Cross Country Cycling Club
54 Highpath Road
Merrow
Guildford, Surrey GU1 2QQ
Great Britain

Countryside Commission
John Dower House
Crescent Place
Cheltenham GL50 3RA
Great Britain

Cyclists' Touring Club
69 Meadrow
Godalming, Surrey GU7 3HS
Great Britain

Effective Cycling League
726 Madrone
Sunnyvale, CA 94086
USA

Mountain Bike Club
J. Torr
3 The Shrubbery
Albert Street
Telford, Shropshire, TF2 9AS
Great Britain

National Park Foundation
PO Box 57473
Washington, DC 20037
USA

National Park Service
U.S. Department of the Interior
18th and C Streets, NW
Room 1013
Washington, DC 20240
USA

NORBA (National Off-Road Bicycle
Association)
P.O. Box 1901
Chandler, AZ 85244

Rough Stuff Fellowship
c/o F.E. Groatcher
65 Stoneleigh Avenue
Worcester Park, Surrey KT4 8XY
Great Britain

Sierra Club
530 Bush Street
San Francisco, CA 94108
USA

United States Forest Service
US Department of Agriculture
P.O. Box 2417
Washington D.C.

US Geological Survey
1200 South Eads Street
Arlington, VA 22202
(map distribution for states east of Mississippi River)

US Geological Survey
P.O. Box 25286
Denver, CO 80225
(map distribution for states west of Mississippi River)

# Periodicals

Adventure Bike
1127 Hamilton Street
Allentown, PA 18102
USA

Bicycle Action
136/138 New Cavendish Street
London W1M 7FG
Great Britain

Bicycle Magazine
PO Box 381
Mill Harbour
London E14 9TW
Great Britain

Making Tracks
Sue Hopkins
55 Grafton Road
New Malden, Surrey KT3 3AA
Great Britain

Rough Stuff Journal
A. J. Matthews
9 Liverpool Avenue
Southport, Merseyside PR8 3NE
Great Britain

Bicycle Times
26 Commercial Bldgs.
Dunston
Tyne and Wear NE11 9AA
Great Britain

Bicycle Guide
711 Boylston St.
Boston, MA 02116
USA

Bicycling
33 E. Minor St.
Emmaus, PA 18049
USA

Cyclist
P.O. Box 907
Farmingdale, NY 11737-0001
USA

Fat Tire Flyer
P.O. Box 757
Fairfax, CA 94930
USA

Mountain Bike
Box 989
Crested Butte, CO 81224
USA

Mountain Bike Action
P.O. Box 9502
Mission Hills, CA 91345-9502
USA

Mountain Biking
7950 Deering Ave.
Canoga Park, CA 91304
USA

# Bibliography

*Advanced First Aid*. New York: Doubleday The American National Red Cross, 1973.

*American Youth Hostels Handbook*. Delaplane, VT: American Youth Hostel Association, (annual).

Ballantine, R., *Richard's Bicycle Book*. New York: Ballantine, London: Pan, 1978.

*Bicycle Touring Atlas*. New York: American Youth Hostel Association, 1969.

Biestman, M., *Travel for Two*: Sausalito, CA: Pergot Press, 1986.

Bridge, R., *Freewheeling: The Bicycle Camping Book*. Harrisonburg, PA: Stackpole Books, 1974.

–, *Bike Touring*. San Francisco: Sierra Club Books, 1979.

Bunelle, H. and Sarvis, S., *Cooking for Camp and Trail*. San Francisco: Sierra Club Books, 1984.

Campground and Trailer Park Guide. Chicago: Rand McNally, (annual).

Carlson, R. (ed), *National Directory of Budget Motels*. New York: Pilot Books, (annual).

*Climates of the States*. Port Washington, NY: United States National Oceanic and Atmospheric Administration, 1974.

Coello, D., *The Mountain Bike Manual*. Salt Lake City, Dream Garden Press 1985.

Coles, C. W., and Glenn, H. T., *Glenn's Complete Bicycle Manual*. New York: Crown Publishers, 1973.

*The Complete Guide to America's National Parks*. Washington, DC: The National Park Foundation, 1984.

*The CTC Handbook*. Godalming, Surrey (GB): Cyclist's Touring Club, (annual).

Cuthberson, T., *Anybody's Bike Book*. Berkeley, CA: Ten-Speed Press, 1984.

–, *Bike Tripping*. Berkeley, CA: Ten-Speed Press, 1984.

DeLong, F., *DeLong's Guide to Bicycles and Bicycling*. Radnor, PA.:Chilton Books, 1978.

Eastman, P.F., *Advanced First Aid for All Outdoors*. Centerville, MD: Cornell Maritime Press, 1976.

Editors of Bicycling Magazine, *Best Bicycle Tours*. Emmaus, PA: Rodale Press, 1981.

Faria, I.E., *Cycling Physiology for the Serious Cyclist*. Springfield, MS: Thomas, 1978.

Fletcher, C., *The New Complete Walker*. New York: Knopf, 1974.

Food and Nutrition Board, *Recommended Dietary Allowances*. Washington, DC: National Academy of Sciences, 1974.

Forester, J., *Effective Cycling*. Cambridge, MS: MIT-Press, 1984.

Gatty, H., *Finding Your Way on Land and Sea*. Brattleboro, VT: Stephen Green Press, 1983

Gausden, C. and Crane, N., *The CTC Route Guide to Cycling in Britain and Ireland*. Oxford: Oxford Illustrated Press, Harmondsworth: Penguin Books, 1980

Greenhood, D, *Mapping*. Chicago: University of Chicago Press, 1964.

Hefferson, L., *Cycle Food*. Berkeley, CA: Ten Speed Press, 1976.

Howard, J., *The Cyclist's Companion*. Brattleboro, VT: Stephen Green Press, 1984.

*Inside the Cyclist*. Brattleboro, VT: Velo-news, 1984.

*International Bicycle Touring*. Mountain View, CA: World Publications, 1976

Kals, W. S., *Land Navigation Handbook*. San Francisco: Sierra Club Books, 1971

Keefe, M., *The Ten Speed Commandments*, Garden City, NY: Doubleday, 1987.

Kellstrom, G., *Map and Compass*. New York: Charles Scribner's Sons, 1973.

Lynn, I. et al, *The Off-Road Bicycle Book*. Butterset (GB): The Leading Edge, 1987.

*National Atlas of the United States*. Washington, DC: US Department of the Interior, Geological Survey, 1970.

Rafoth, R., *Bicycling Fuel*, San Francisco: Bicycle Books, 1988.

Rostaing, B. and Walton, B., *Bill Walton's Total Book of Bicycling*. New York, Toronto: Bantam Books, 1985.

Sloane, E., *Eugene A. Sloane's Complete Guide to All-Terrain Bicycles*. New York: Simon & Schuster 1985.

–, *The New Complete Book of Bicycling*. New York: Simon & Schuster, 1981.

Thomas, D., *Roughing it Easy*. Provo, UT: Brigham Young University Press, 1974.

Van der Plas, R., *The Bicycle Commuting Book*. San Francisco: Bicycle Books, 1988.

–, *The Bicycle Racing Guide*. San Francisco: Bicycle Books, 1986.

–, *The Bicycle Repair Book*. San Francisco: Bicycle Books, 1985.

–, *The Bicycle Touring Manual*. San Francisco: Bicycle Books, 1987.

–, *The Penguin Bicycle Handbook*. Harmondsworth (GB): Penguin Books, 1983.

–, *Roadside Bicycle Repairs*. San Francisco: Bicycle Books, 1987.

Watts, A., *Instant Weather Forecasting*. New York: Dodd Mead & Co, 1968.

Whiter, R., *The Bicycle Manual on Maintenance and Repairs*. Chicago, IL: Contemporary Books, 1972.

Whitt, F. R. and Wilson, D. G., *Bicycling Science*. Cambridge, MS: MIT-Press, 1982.

Wilhelm, T. and G., *The Bicycle Touring Book*. Emmaus, PA: Rodale Press, 1980.

# Index

# Other books published by Bicycle Books, Inc.

## The Bicycle Repair Book
The complete manual of bicycle care
by Rob Van der Plas

ISBN 0-933201-11-7
6 x 9 inches, soft cover, 144 pages,
with 300 illustrations.
US price $ 7.95

The most thorough and systematic bicycle repair manual on the market today. It covers all repair and maintenance jobs required on any kind of bicycle. Complete with step-by-step instructions, clear illustrations and an extensive troubleshooting guide.

## The Bicycle Racing Guide
Technique and training for bicycle
racers and triathletes
by Rob Van der Plas

ISBN 0-933201-13-3
6 x 9 inches, soft cover, 256 pages,
with 250 photographs and line drawings.
US price $ 9.95

The most concise and useful book for those who want to increase their cycling speed. Includes an introduction to the sport, as well as complete instructions for scientific training methods and practical advice for racing and training situations.

## Roadside Bicycle Repairs
The simple guide to fixing your bike
by Rob Van der Plas

ISBN 0-933201-16-8
4⅜ x 6 inches, soft cover, 112 pages,
with 120 illustrations.
US price $ 3.95

The book for those who want to fix their bike when they need to – nothing more, nothing less. Systematically arranged and clearly illustrated, this easy-to-follow guide to essential bicycle repairs can be taken along on any trip.

## Major Taylor
The extraordinary career of an early
American champion bicycle racer
by Andrew Ritchie

ISBN 0-933201-14-1
6 x 9 inches, hard cover, 256 pages,
with over 80 photographs.
US price $ 18.95

Beautifully illustrated and vividly told, this is the authentic story of the dramatic life of one of the earliest black American champion athletes. Bicycle racer 'Major' Taylor vanquished his American, European and Australian competitors at home and abroad more than eighty years before Greg LeMond won the Tour de France.

## The Bicycle Touring Manual
Using the bike for touring and
camping
by Rob Van der Plas

ISBN 0-933201-15-X
6 x 9 inches, soft cover, 272 pages,
with 75 photographs and 180 line drawings.
US price $ 9.95

Easily the most useful book for the cyclist who plans to travel by bike. This thorough and well illustrated manual systematically shows you how to select, use and maintain the equipment, how to plan your tour and how to enjoy cycling at home and abroad.

## Bicycling Fuel
Nutrition for bicycle riders
by Richard Rafoth MD

ISBN 0-933201-17-6
4⅜ x 6 inches, soft cover, 128 pages,
with 40 illustrations.
US price $ 3.95

This concise and convenient book is the most authoritative source of nutritional advice for bicycle riders. Shows you what to eat and drink, what to avoid.

All books published by Bicycle Books, Inc. may be obtained through the book or bike trade. If not available locally, use the coupon below to order directly from the publisher:

Bicycle Books, Inc.
P.O.Box 2038
Mill Valley, CA 94941
Tel.: (415) 381 0172

---

☐ Check here if payment enclosed

Please send the following book(s):

| | | |
|---|---|---|
| The Bicycle Repair Book | _____ copies x $ 7.95 | = $ _____ |
| The Mountain Bike Book | _____ copies x $ 8.95 | = $ _____ |
| The Bicycle Racing Guide | _____ copies x $ 9.95 | = $ _____ |
| The Bicycle Touring Manual | _____ copies x $ 9.95 | = $ _____ |
| Roadside Bicycle Repairs | _____ copies x $ 3.95 | = $ _____ |
| Bicycling Fuel | _____ copies x $ 3.95 | = $ _____ |
| Major Taylor | _____ copies x $ 18.95 | = $ _____ |

|  |  |
|---|---|
| Sub total | $ _____ |
| California residents add tax | $ _____ |
| If not paid with order, add $ 1.00 P&H per book | $ _____ |

Total amount                                            $ _____

Name: _____

Address: _____

City, state, zip:_____

Telephone: (_____)_____

Signature: _____  Date: _____

Bicycle Books, Inc. will pay postage and handling if payment in full (check or money order) is enclosed with order form. California residents add tax. If payment does not accompany order, books will be sent COD and customer will be charged for postage and handling at $ 1.00 per copy. Allow three weeks for delivery. Make check or money order payable to Bicycle Books, Inc. and mail to Bicycle Books, Inc., P.O.Box 2038, Mill Valley, CA 94941.